HOW TO SURVIVE
FEDERAL PRISON CAMP
A Guidebook For Those
Caught Up In The System

HOW TO SURVIVE FEDERAL PRISON CAMP
A Guidebook For Those Caught Up In The System

by Clive Sharp

Loompanics Unlimited
Port Townsend, Washington

This book is sold for informational purposes only. Neither the author nor the publisher will be held accountable for the use or misuse of the information contained in this book.

HOW TO SURVIVE FEDERAL PRISON
A Guidebook For Those Caught Up In The System
© 1997 by Clive Sharp

Published by:
Loompanics Unlimited
PO Box 1197
Port Townsend, WA 98368
Loompanics Unlimited is a division of Loompanics Enterprises, Inc.
1-360-385-2230

Cover photo courtesy U.S. Bureau of Prisons
Illustrations by Holly K. Tuttle

ISBN 1-55950-167-7
Library of Congress Card Catalog 97-74040

CONTENTS

INTRODUCTION
BY CLAIRE WOLFE

Welcome to FFA. No, not Future Farmers of America, that pleasant little relic of the days when America was the land of the free.

I'm talking about Future Felons of America, the club to which millions of us now belong. Our membership is growing by leaps, bounds and midnight kicks on our doors. You may not want to be part of this contemporary American FFA. (Who in their right mind would?) But it's best to face facts; in a country where would-be rulers, elected and unelected, are desperate to regulate every activity, we are all law-breakers or soon to become so.

You and I, friends, are likely to end up in prison.

Worse, we're increasingly likely to end up in the custody of the federal prison system. Activities that were once the business of the states — or nobody's business but your own — are being taken over by control freaks in Washington, DC, whose favorite masturbatory fantasy is that they can micro-manage every human activity 24 hours a day and punish everyone who deviates from their desires. That means your chances of going to federal prison — or a federal prison camp like the ones described in this book — are getting "better" every day.

Here are just a few of the "crimes" that can already land you in the federal system:

- Taking one prescription pill out of its drugstore bottle and carrying it around in a different container. (Just think of all those dangerous, blue-haired old lady felons lurking in *your* neighborhood with pills stashed in daily-dose containers from their local Wal-Mart!)
- Making a mistake on an Environmental Protection Agency reporting form — even if everyone agrees it was just a mistake and that no pollution was involved.
- Driving past a school with an otherwise perfectly legal gun in your car — even driving a block away from a school you didn't know was there!
- Manufacturing or selling a container that someone *might* use to store illegal drugs. (Kinda makes you wonder why Wal-Mart doesn't get busted for selling "drug paraphernalia" to those blue-haired ladies, doesn't it?)
- Digging dinosaur bones if you're not a university professor or government employee.
- Putting a picture of a naked lady on a wine bottle label (unless an ATF agent decides it's "art," which automatically makes it okay).
- Sitting in the car while an acquaintance goes into a house to do a drug deal.

This last one comes under the heading of "conspiracy." And conspiracy is one of a raft of ill-defined "crimes" the feds are using as a catch-all for anyone they want to bag. In addition to "conspiring" by doing nothing, you might be accused of "violating someone's civil rights" by punching him in the nose or "participating in organized criminal activity" just for talking about the wrong subject or being in the wrong place with the wrong people.

What organized criminal activity does this latter charge refer to? Don't ask. If the government had an actual crime — like murder or robbery — to charge you with, believe me, they would. "Participating in organized criminal activity" simply means you've gotten together with your buddies and done something a bureaucrat doesn't like.

The feds can *always* find you guilty of something. If they want to.

THE REAL REASON FOR ALL THOSE LAWS

And that's the rub. *If they want to.* Because these laws, of course, aren't designed to stop evildoers at all. They're designed to allow selective control of people who make waves, deviate from convention, own independent businesses, criticize unjust authority, and otherwise insist on living their lives as they see fit. Or they're designed to let enforcers arrest a lot of people so they can brag about their successes in "fighting crime" — and so they can confiscate valuable private property under the hundreds of new and existing civil forfeiture laws.

No one really seems to know how many federal laws and regulations we're living under today, but five million pages is the most reliable number I've heard. (Eleven million pages of combined state and federal legis-regulation.) The silly federal "crimes" mentioned above don't even begin to scratch the surface of the pointless, harmless things for which you can be sent to prison.

And the control freaks are cranking out new crimes at the rate of 200 pages a day!

Two hundred pages a day. Now, obviously, all the violent, nasty, fraudulent stuff was made illegal a hundred or more years ago. Protections against murder, armed robbery, fraud, rape and such are basics and were taken care of by the people and the states long before any of us were born. Even new technology and changing times haven't really brought about the need for defining new crimes. Theft by computer is still theft and is covered by laws made long, long ago. Rape by battery operated dildo is still rape. Homicide by genetically engineered toxin is still homicide.

Even when you consider truly new things some government *might* need to deal with (like, maybe, disposal of nuclear wastes), there simply can't be any legitimate reason for the volume of legis-regulation spewing out of Washington, DC, and the state capitals today.

Ayn Rand said it best in her novel, *Atlas Shrugged*: "There is no way to rule innocent men. The only power government has is the power to crack down on criminals. Well, when there aren't enough criminals, one makes them. One declares so many things to be a crime that it becomes impossible for men to live without breaking laws."

And that's the way it is in America today. And getting worse.

DON'T EXPECT JUSTICE

I know it's considered silly and naïve these days to mention the U.S. Constitution. As Douglas Wilder, a recent governor of Virginia, said, "I don't care what those men wrote 200 years ago." And as Bill Clinton famously added, the founders of this country were too radical and the government now has to move to limit freedom. Maybe you don't care about the

Constitution, either. You, as a private individual, don't have to. It wasn't written to tell *you* what you can or can't do.

However, that beleaguered old document is still the supreme law of the land, which every government agent has pledged to obey. And nowhere does the Constitution give the federal government any authority over crimes, other than counterfeiting, treason, and unspecified crimes that occur outside the territory of the states. Since it's quite clear from Amendments 9 and 10 that the federal government has *only* those powers specifically delegated to it by the Constitution, the hundreds of thousands of federal laws on the books and the thousands of new pages being passed by Congress and their regulatory co-conspirators every year are illegal as hell. Just about every one of them.

Isn't that interesting? Every time some marshal, DEA agent, ATF agent or other masked, black-clad fedgoon arrests you for a federal "crime," he really ought to be arrested himself!

But, of course, that isn't going to happen. Because all that matters today is power, not justice, not fundamental principles of law. The Congresscreature who makes tyrannical laws is never going to be forced to pay for its crimes. The judge who enforces bad laws and lies to juries about their rights is never going to pay for the destruction she wreaks upon people. The fedgoon is never, never, never going to be called to account for his rampages. (Remember that Deputy U.S. Marshal Larry Cooper got a reward for shooting Sammy Weaver in the back, Lon Horiuchi was slipped into the Witness Protection Program as a reward for murdering Sammy's mother, and not a single agent has paid for the mass murder of the Branch Davidians. Besides which, damnit all, no president of the United States has gone to prison yet.)

The president of Wal-Mart isn't going to get busted for selling plastic pill boxes to the bluehairs, either. And it's not because Wal-Mart, that quite likable store, is merely pursuing peaceful, legitimate business activity for which no one in a free society could ever be busted. Remember, that doesn't matter any more. What matters to the feds is that Wal-Mart is rich, powerful and politically connected. It knows how to play the government game. It pays its "regulatory fees," its "permits" and its other forms of tribute (legal bribery) to the powers-that-be. It goes along to get along. Its executives hobnob with politicians and no doubt "donate" $10,000 per plate for rubber chicken at political fundraisers in order to be allowed to survive in a burgeoning police state.

But a poor immigrant can — and did — go to federal prison for making bottles someone *might* have been able to use to store crack cocaine, even though he had no knowledge of, or connection with, such use. He didn't have connections. He didn't grease the palms of the right government bureaucrats. So he was fair game for goons and their pet judges.

Modern America is divided into those who are above the law, those who manage to squeak their way around the law — and those who can, at any moment, be crushed by the law. Like you and me.

Don't expect fairness. Don't expect justice. Just grit your teeth, strengthen your gut and get ready to survive when it happens to you. If you're lucky, if you're really lucky, you'll end up in a mere prison camp instead of a hardcore prison, and your mental and physical survival job will be a little easier.

LISTEN TO THOSE WHO'VE BEEN THERE

I haven't been in federal prison. Nor any prison. I've never even spent a night in the county jail. Heck, I haven't even had a speeding ticket in ten years! (Though I did get that on the Interstate. Hmmm, I wonder why Congress hasn't thought of making speeding on the Interstate a federal felony — yet?) I am your stereotypical law-abiding citizen—or would be if such a thing were possible in America today.

So why should you listen to me when it comes to surviving federal prison camp? One answer is: you shouldn't. You shouldn't listen to anybody. Any-*one*-body, that is. To prepare yourself, you should find out as much as possible from as many different sources as possible. Listen to Clive Sharp, who wrote this book and offers his prison-survival advice in a cool, "just the facts, Ma'am," manner.

Listen to Donald B. Parker, whose words appear after mine and again at the end of this book; he speaks with the voice of multiple experience.

Listen to Dr. Reinhold Aman, in his book *Hillary Clinton's Pen Pal*, who turns his federal-prison bitterness into some of the sharpest-humored words ever written about incarceration.

Listen to G. Gordon Liddy (*Will*). Listen to Jim Hogshire, whose book *You Are Going to Prison* explains with gut & grit how to survive most any prison experience. Read Norma Jean Almodovar's harrowing, saucy and brave *Cop to Callgirl*, which details her experiences in the Los Angeles Jail and the California prison system. Read and learn to prepare for your own future, in whatever prison system you may end up.

Though I haven't been in prison myself, friends and acquaintances have. They got there mostly because they talked to the wrong people about the wrong subjects (political ones) at the wrong time.

Some got conned by federal informants, posing as friends, into violating rules and regulations.

Some of them got there as casualties in the War Against (Some) Drugs.

A few got there because they wouldn't yield on principles — a fatally unfashionable thing to do, these days.

As I admitted, I'm a Goody Two-Shoes at heart; I don't hang out with lowlifes. These are terrific people I'm talking about here. Smart, hard-working individuals with creative hearts, strong principles and independent streaks a mile wide.

Exactly the kind of people a sensible government would respect and leave alone.

Exactly the kind of people who build strong communities and strong nations. But because they've refused to bow to the obsessive wishes of control freaks, they've been ripped from their jobs, families and lives.

- I'm talking about a Ph.D microbiologist, yanked out of his research lab and pitched into a camp for years, where he gets to do nothing more productive than wash dirty laundry.
- I'm talking about a good mother, ripped away from her children because her religion forbids her to pay income taxes, forced to watch from a distance as those children grow up motherless, fatherless, and filled with bursting rage.
- I'm talking about a business man, branded a "racketeer" so that the government could seize his home, trucks and bank account. He once employed 11 people. Now he sits in a cell, just trying to occupy his time so that he doesn't

go nuts. His wife has since left him — as most wives of convicts do.

- I'm talking about a father of four, thrown into jail, wife and son shot dead by federal officers, surviving children hustled into the custody of relatives.

These folks never hurt anybody. But they have been and are being hurt — as you will be. They relate experiences we'd probably rather not think about:

- They tell of being put under "suicide watch." Oh, yeah, that sounds humane. What it really means is that voyeurs with video cameras get to watch you piss, shit, play with yourself, or however else you manage to spend your days. It's all part of the process of breaking down your will, of reminding you that your entire life is now under *their* control.

- My friends tell of solitary confinement. Solitary always sounded like a relatively good thing to me, since I have the soul of a monk. But picture "solitary" not meaning one, but two — two prisoners lying on the concrete floor of a windowless, unfurnished 4 x 10 cell, with one prisoner screaming night and day, throwing himself against the walls. Maybe throwing himself at *you* in his fits of insane, irrational loathing. Picture being put in this coffin-space with this madman for days simply because you stood up for your own rights.

- They tell of having the clothes and spending money they brought to prison unaccountably "lost" by prison personnel.

- They tell of waiting days, weeks, months for medical treatment. (*Never* believe the idiots who are so jealous of convicts' "free medical care"!)

- They tell of earning 11 cents per hour working behind the walls for profit-making U.S. corporations. Hey, not many of us are against businesses making money. But isn't there something called slave labor? Don't we damn countries like China for producing goods that way? (Mark my words, this little-known, but growing, alliance between prisons and corporations is another important reason for the boom in prison building and law spewing. Convicts make a handy-dandy — literally captive — work force. And don't imagine your local congressbeast isn't discussing this happy possibility with the president of your local mega-corporation right now.)

- The political prisoners — those who have media and Internet contacts on the outside — tell the worst tales of all. They relate with shudders and fury their experience of Diesel Therapy. Both Clive Sharp and Donald B. Parker mention Diesel Therapy elsewhere in this book, so I won't dwell on it. But rest assured, those who've endured it say it's worse than anyone could describe. Picture spending up to six months on a bus, shackled hand, foot and waist, not even able to take down your own pants without a struggle or wipe your own butt clean at a rest stop. You never know where you're going. You're not able to let your family or friends know where you are. You have no way of knowing when the endless trip will cease. You have no access to your own books, paper, pencils or stamps. Back and forth across the country you go, in all kinds of temperatures and conditions, on an endless journey to nowhere — all so that you won't be able to get word to those on the outside who might help publicize your case. And they say there's no cruel and unusual punishment allowed in America!

Even if you "behave," that doesn't mean you'll have it easy. Simple, everyday things can be almost unendurable. I remember phone conversations with one friend who served more than a year in county jail while awaiting his trial, sentencing and transfer to the federal system. He would call me collect from a common room. The level of noise behind him was such that we had to shout at each other to be heard. And in nearly every conversation, there was another prisoner, very near him, yipping and howling like a dog for hours. Yipping and howling at full, dog-pound volume.

My friend endured this philosophically. I remember thinking at the time that I would scream, myself, if I had to listen to that much longer.

Someday, I may have to listen to that, or something like it. Maybe listen for years. As I sit here typing this in the beauty of a spring-green garden, with two gentle dogs at my feet and my true love nearby, it's nearly inconceivable. I lead a peaceful life, and I wish with all my heart to keep this joy until my last breath on earth.

But every day I — like you — harmlessly violate some unknown number of federal laws or regulations. And I — like a growing number of others — speak out loudly and often against the injustices of an out-of-control government. So I have to face the fact that, someday, the Sauron-Eye of Washington, DC will turn in my direction.

On that day, if the stormtroopers of some multi-agency task force are too lazy to find actual violations on which to grab me, it will be easy enough for them to twist free speech into "conspiracy" or to fake evidence of criminal activity. (Another useful by-product of the War on (Some) Drugs — just grab a little dope or "meth lab equipment" out of the evidence room and plant it on anybody you don't like.)

And on that day, my friend, when they've reached the point of rounding up little ladies guilty mainly of having fierce opinions, a lot of you fine readers will already be "inside." I hope we're all prepared.

FOREWORD
BY DONALD B. PARKER

Perhaps the most important thing for a person to keep in mind upon preparing to enter a federal prison camp is you are no longer operating in a rational environment (not that the one you're leaving necessarily is). To expect reasonable responses or solutions to given situations or problems is to invite frustration. There will be no meaningful dialogue between you and your jailers. It will be a monologue, and you are to do as you're told. When it comes right down to it, this experience will be all about behavior modification.

What little pretense about prison "rehabilitation" that existed in previous eras is no longer in effect. This is the time of the "no frills" prison experience, and fewer and fewer "amenities" are available to members of the convicted class. The direction things are going is definitely less, not more; subtraction, not addition.

The ideal demeanor for a convict who hopes to survive federal prison camp is exemplified by becoming inconspicuous. If possible, the convict should strive to be the sort of person whose name doesn't register in the guards' minds when, after five years of incarceration, he is preparing to walk out the door. Anonymity is the condition one wishes to achieve. The fewer times your name comes up, the better off you will be.

You must ask yourself, "What exactly does 'surviving federal prison camp' mean to me?" If you come into the prison camp thinking the best way to handle the experience is to sleep as much as possible and generally zone out, you are courting disaster. To borrow a phrase, "This is not a rehearsal. This is your life!" Your time in the prison camp will be a "time out" of sorts, but it will also be a very special opportunity to examine your life and look at the issues surrounding you and your characteristics, factors which clearly haven't generated positive results in the past.

In a fundamentally inhospitable, threatening, and anti-humanistic environment, a habitat that insidiously eats away at the parts of you that are alive, caring, and life-affirming, one has to pay even more attention to one's surroundings than is usually necessary in everyday civilian life. There is so little ambient stimulation that it becomes all too easy to go to sleep and lose the mental edge and connection with life that we experience more easily in the "real" world. Make no mistake about it, this is a warehouse situation and, as mentioned above, rehabilitation is a concept which is no longer in favor.

Your sojourn in federal prison camp can be a tremendous opportunity to achieve a level of discipline and self-awareness that may have been missing in your life. For those coming into the system who are used to solving their problems by throwing money at them, or giving orders and being catered to, or to living an aristocratic lifestyle, it will be necessary to learn many new survival skills.

Money spent in the right places and the right way can make your stay easier. There are people who, for a fee, will do your laundry, work at your job, tailor your clothes, and furnish and cook your food. If you're going to participate in this "black market" unofficial economy, do so quietly and with a certain humility. At the same time you are helping someone out by providing them with an opportunity to earn money, you are also arousing the envy and jealousy of someone who would like to enjoy the same service(s) but can't afford it. Because everything that goes on in camp does so underneath an invisible magnifying glass, it's important to keep this aspect of your incarceration in mind as you go about your business.

A federal prison camp is truly like a small village, in that everyone knows everybody else's business. It is also a lot like the party game in which a message is whispered from person to person, and becomes completely distorted (sometimes beyond recognition) by the time the original information reaches the last person.

This aspect of the prison-camp experience lends extra weight to the next "survival" rule, which is so obvious and essential that it bears repeating: **Do not speak openly or frankly about your net worth. To the best of your ability, "poor mouth" your financial situation.** Even though you are in a camp and not a higher security-level facility, you are in the midst of plenty of desperate, angry people, many of whom have led and still lead predatory existences. "Gang bangers" are often heard talking about "taking people off" (robbing those) whom they suspected were worth a lot of money. The last thing you want to worry about is some money-hungry, conscienceless gangster sizing you up for his personal financial enrichment.

Additionally, if the popular perception of you is that you've got a lot of money, the likelihood of your getting hit up for loans and tips on how to get rich increases dramatically. There are plenty of white-collar types in the camps these days, many "former millionaires" (by their own descriptions) and high rollers who, at any given time, have two or three "can't miss" financial opportunities on their plates. When you can no longer resist the urge to listen to one of these undeniably enticing propositions, force yourself to exercise common sense and not get sucked in before you've really done your homework. Also, keep in mind that you're not allowed to enter into any business dealings with your new "colleagues" without the authorities' permission.

However, in the interest of presenting a more balanced point of view, there **are** a number of bright, articulate types with a wealth of information, education, and experience at their disposal, from whom one can learn vital information if so inclined. You must simply be patient and take the time to ferret out such individuals.

As difficult to do as it may be after you've been clobbered by your arrest and it looks as if your life is headed for the toilet, put your affairs in order to the best of your ability. This may seem awfully obvious, but while you're awaiting the outcome of your legal problems (pre-trial/presentencing), it is extremely easy to seize up in the free-will department and generally become paralyzed. When you're looking at the hard end of life as you've known it and you're standing at the brink of the abyss, it is essentially all too easy to give up or adopt an "eat, drink, and be merry" attitude. This may momentarily make the pain go away, but it will not make your time, and that of the people you love and will be leaving behind (and whom you are responsible for), any easier or more manageable.

Being in prison is a lot like planning to run a race. If you've got a short sentence — six months to two years — your perception of how to handle things and what you're going to do is going to be very different from that of someone looking at five to ten years. It's a lot like the difference between a sprint and a long-distance run.

People with short sentences are looked upon with a certain amount of disdain, indifference, and distrust by those unfortunates who are serving long sentences. These long-timers often become "time snobs." Guys with big time really don't want to hear about how difficult things are from guys with short sentences, and tend to discount anything short-timers have to say about the "prison experience." They simply don't feel these people have earned the right to talk, and the often unstated inference is that short-timers are more likely to be snitches.

And then there are the staff. For all intents and purposes, the staff view you as severely damaged goods, and take your circumstances as justification to treat you like vermin. One of my favorite exchanges with a guard was when he asked naïve, freshly enlisted me, "How do you know when an inmate is lying?" When I responded that I didn't know, he answered, "When his lips are moving." (By the way, the staff insist on labeling the prisoners as "inmates," while many prisoners prefer to be known as "convicts." This is a very important distinction to some people, and it should be taken seriously.)

It is generally believed by convicts that, as a group, the staff (hacks [guards], administrators, etc.) are not employable in the private sector, largely because of gross stupidity and ineptitude. In many prisons and prison camps, there are a curiously large number of staff who have gone directly from the armed forces to the penal quagmire. This doesn't appear to be purely coincidental. The affinity between the military and penal mentality is undeniable.

The preeminent concern and governing principal that lies at the foundation of all prison staff behavior is the importance of "job security," which is primarily characterized by a servile attitude towards one's superiors, and ardent passing of the buck to the staff person with even less power who is lower in the chain of command. Ethical considerations, humanistic impulses, and any of the other qualities that supposedly differentiate civilized people from unfeeling thugs go right out the window if job security is in any way threatened.

While an anecdote or two can probably be gleaned from the hoary annals of penal history, the number of times a hack has taken the side of or backed up a convict in an encounter with another hack are few and far between. "Stand by your man (or woman)" right or wrong is, I suspect, part of the oath hacks take when they are inducted into the prison guards' union. It is impossible for a convict to win an argument with a hack. They will lie and misinterpret a situation to serve their own ends, and not those of justice. Hard to believe, I know, but absolutely true.

It's important not to develop any illusions about forming friendships or normal relations with staff. Over time, it's easy and natural to forget that staff are first and foremost employees of the Bureau of Prisons (BOP), that their primary concern is job security, and that what is right or just is clearly secondary to what is self-serving, expedient, and preserves job security. If at all possible, do not allow yourself to engage in a one-on-one conversation with a hack. It is better to have other convicts present when speaking with a hack. That is because many of your fellow convicts are very paranoid, and fear and loathe snitches above all other beings. They will often assume that if you are talking to a hack one-on-one, you are a snitch delivering information. This assumption, erroneous or not, can result in your disfigurement or death.

Many hacks, during those occasional moments when they let their hair down and speak honestly, will talk about the hypocrisy, illogic, and stupidity of the system, and how they feel like insignificant cogs in a big machine. But when it comes time to do something that they don't really believe in, the hacks just swallow hard and go ahead and do as they are told.

This fundamental dishonesty in relationships is tolerable with the normal jailers and is pretty much to be expected. It's very difficult when the staff psychologist or physician, both of whom are doctors who have taken the Hippocratic oath, remind a convict that the practitioner's allegiance is first and foremost to the institution, and secondly to their patients. The convict is expected to speak from the heart and reveal his fundamental concerns and thoughts to people who listen to what he has to say through a very special filter that limits their ability to do what is best for him. **Be extremely careful and circumspect about what you say to the staff psychologist**. He is primarily concerned with identifying and weeding out anyone who sounds as if he might pose a threat to the security of the camp. This concern sounds benign on the surface, but can easily be interpreted in a way that could justify shipping you out or sending you to a penal setting that is better equipped to handle your particular sort of "problem" — for example, Springfield, where extreme medical/mental cases are typically confined.

My experience in the spiritual realm — the chapel and the chaplains — was equally disappointing, and followed the same "BOP first" guiding principle. The answer to the question, "Do you serve God or Caesar first?" was quite clear. In the course of my stay we had three chaplains, only one of which fit the model of a spiritual mentor, and he quit out of disillusionment with the administration. The two who followed him were toadies in the truest sense of the word, and neither displayed the slightest evidence of a spiritual aspect.

How To Survive Federal Prison Camp

XX

The overarching mind-set and ethos was that we, as felons, had truly fallen from both secular and spiritual grace, that we were tainted, damaged goods, and that we were to be treated accordingly. I often felt like a child being reprimanded, who is ordered to stand in the corner and face the wall.

All journeys have a beginning and an end, and for the purpose inherent in this book, your incarnation as a survivor in a federal prison camp begins with your arrival at the facility. When you first arrive, no matter if you're a self-surrenderer or have been delivered from a county jail or somewhere else within the gulag, you will sport a characteristic gray pallor reminiscent of someone who has seen something too awful to describe. The shock to your system that comes from surrendering your freedom for an unimaginable length of time puts you on the fritz. In addition to the change in skin tone, one can expect to undergo gastrointestinal adjustments that can go on for months as your body struggles to get in tune with the new dietary order. Obviously, the healthier and younger you are when you enter the camp, the easier the physical stresses should be.

If there are any items of clothing you can somehow manage to finagle in when passing through Reception and Indoctrination (R&D), definitely opt for the most comfortable pair(s) of shoes and good-quality cotton socks you can convince the hacks to be absolutely necessary. The quality of shoes and socks supplied by the BOP is marginal at best.

Also, try to get the largest bath towel possible in as well. The towels supplied are a maximum of 36" long, making it extremely difficult to wrap around your expanding waist as you leave the shower.

If you're a contact-lens wearer, bring in the largest bottle of wetting and cleaning solution available on the market, since acquiring further supplies involves a special order which, more likely than not, will be fraught with problems and delays. Bring spare contact lenses and reading glasses. You can get free eyeglasses courtesy of the BOP. The frames you'll have to choose from are arguably the ugliest you will have ever seen, so if fashion is one of your priorities, you'll want to keep this in mind. The BOP will not provide you with contact lenses.

It is possible to smuggle items into the camp, but I strongly advise against it. There is really nothing that you can't live without, excluding medicine, that is worth chancing additional sanctions (getting shipped, picking up another charge, doing time in the hole). In addition to getting yourself in a jam, the person who smuggled the goods can also be charged with introducing contraband to a federal reservation and get into serious trouble. Guys who have their old ladies smuggle in dope and thereby put them at serious risk are real jerks. Furthermore, since everyone is aware of everyone else's business, anyone who shows up out of the blue with fresh supplies of this or that immediately becomes grist for the snitch mill, and not infrequently earns the jealousy of those less fortunate inmates who have neither the money for extra "outside" luxuries nor anyone willing to bring them into the prison.

There are snitches so ridiculously eager to curry favor with the police that they are all too willing to drop a dime on you if you turn up with an unregistered bar of soap or a new unauthorized pair of shoes. Even if you don't get caught, you are certainly going to draw attention to yourself and make yourself subject to frequent shakedowns and the undesired scrutiny of the Man.

Matters of health should be weighed very carefully. The medical attention you'll get is marginal at best. The typical response for all ailments short of death throes is Motrin and bed rest. This is not hyperbole. In the three years I was down, five people died, four of whom could definitely have been saved had there been adequate response time, medical awareness on the part of the hacks, and, in one case, the appropriate medication. One lives with the knowledge that unless you are manifesting unmistakable signs of medical distress — bleeding profusely, bone(s) protruding from skin, doubled over in pain with inexplicable and copious amounts of sweat — you're "fucked." Guys who broke bones during a Friday evening baseball game had to wait until Monday to get medical attention, because there was no physician's assistant (p.a.) on the weekend — just pill line. Two guys who complained of chest pains earlier in the evening (both of whom had histories of heart problems) were sent back to their bunks, told to take aspirin and rest, and had heart attacks later in the evening. One died.

In the dental realm, tooth removal is the all-too-frequent response to tooth problems. People who spent a lot of money on their teeth while civilians and have the proof in evidence in their mouths (lots of gold fillings) seem to get a less automatically indifferent response to their dental problems than those inmates whose mouths demonstrate poor dental hygiene and general inattention to the care of their teeth. If the dentist looks into your mouth and sees a cesspool with stumps, he's going to exhibit about the same level of concern as you obviously did. The moment you get into camp and see the dentist during the standard intake physical, **make an appointment to have your teeth cleaned.** You will be placed on a list, and in roughly six months you'll visit the dentist for a cleaning. **If at all possible, have all your dental work, including a cleaning, done before you arrive at camp. Talk to your dentist and have him tell you if any of your teeth might conceivably need to come out in whatever the**

duration of your time to be served is estimated to be. Be clear on this, because removal is definitely a preferred (because it's cheaper) response on the BOP's part.

On the brighter side of this medical reality, I saw some excellent work done in the realm of hernias (of which there were many produced by overzealous weight lifters), scoped knees, and a quadruple bypass surgery. These operations were all performed at a local hospital by apparently competent surgeons. The only criticism of these procedures was that they generally took place quite a while after the recipients were identified as requiring surgery. Those who underwent hernia surgeries were also sent home the day the operations were performed, which is probably not typical.

If you are a vegetarian, prepare yourself for a pretty meager dietary experience. You'll see a lot of kidney beans, vegetarian baked beans, and iceberg lettuce. You'll also get part of an onion, green pepper, and tomato with lunch and dinner (the availability depending on locale and funding). Any vegetarian who survives on this fare receives the distinguished vegetarian cross and is guaranteed direct transmission to the big garden in the sky when he vacates this mortal coil.

Another factor to consider is visiting-room protocol. The range of things one can and cannot do in the visiting room varies from camp to camp, but, as with everything else within the current BOP, the trend is toward less, rather than more. My experience and that of veterans of other camps describes a similar and fundamentally sterile setting. There is "furniture" which affords the opportunity for very little intimacy. There are no individual chairs which would allow you to form circles of chairs or face each other while conversing. The available food comes from vending machines, and its outstanding feature would have to be its remarkable shelf life, closely followed by the truly amazing number of chemical additives present in each tasty offering. Anyone with the most rudimentary interest in health and nutrition will have nothing from which to choose, and your guests are not allowed to bring in any food. Children are not permitted to bring in any toys or books, but occasionally a kindly visiting-room hack will turn a blind eye.

The rules for touching between men and women are basically the allowance of one decent kiss and/or embrace at the beginning and end of the visit. General groping and any sexually suggestive behavior is uniformly forbidden, even though one guard's parameters and tolerance may vary considerably from another's. While some guards think of themselves as soldiers in the Army for a Sexually Abstinent America, most guards are more concerned with the prospect of your irate grandmother writing a letter to the warden complaining about being forced to watch some barbarian and his consort performing unmistakably sexual acts in front of her and her five fascinated grandchildren. This makes the guard look derelict in the performance of his duty, which ultimately threatens his job security and income. Remember, job security is at the top of every BOP employee's list of essential criteria.

Furthermore, whenever one of these unsavory incidents takes place and the visiting-room guard is reprimanded, the usual response is a reign of terror which translates into a visiting-room atmosphere so repressive that you might as well blow off getting any visits until the reprimanded guard gets rotated out and is replaced by a (hopefully) more benign presence. Also, when all the other convicts find out that your selfish need to have your wife give you a blow job has ruined visiting privileges for everyone else, you will be branded as an asshole and generally despised. On the bright side, your act of public sexuality will probably raise your stock enormously amongst those who think it's really cool to treat women as sperm receptacles, and, God knows, there are plenty in every camp who hold that opinion. It's your call.

Among the most daunting issues you'll face is how to maintain meaningful, vital relationships with people you love, such as your wife, children, parents, and extended family. Like so many other issues you'll be forced to confront, the successful handling of personal relationships will be affected in no small way by the amount of time you have to serve.

The likelihood of your remaining married and connected to your primary loved ones undoubtedly decreases with each year that goes by, and as a percentage, the number of marriages that survive a lengthy sentence is very small. This is sad but true. Couples with children appear to do better than those without, but this is certainly not an offhand way of encouraging couples who are about to undergo the debacle of incarceration to have a baby. One of the most painful sights one can see is a visiting room full of infants whose fathers were already incarcerated before their birth or shortly thereafter.

Some camps have parenting classes, and if you're fortunate to have a teacher who has prepared good materials and actually cares about the subject matter, you can definitely improve your parenting skills and learn some useful, enjoyable ways to connect with your children. If nothing else, participation in a structured environment which focuses on this specific dilemma — how to parent a child from within a prison — is a very worthwhile thing to do. It's simply too easy to neglect this painful but all-important aspect of your life. Getting in the habit of writing to your children once a week or even more frequently will serve them and you very well. Receiving messages from their father on a regular, dependable basis will help keep you alive in their hearts and minds. Don't get so overly concerned with the quality of your letters that you don't send anything. This is one instance where quantity is every bit as important as quality.

As with so many things in life, you'll get out of it what you put into it, or, to borrow a hackneyed phrase, "garbage in, garbage out." The convicts who have the most solid and enduring relationships with both their wives and children are, in most cases, the ones who have invested time and energy in their families before they were arrested. What a surprise! If your girlfriend or wife is basically a high-maintenance party girl with champagne tastes, someone who is used to being taken care of and having lots of money to throw at life's problems, the likelihood of her sticking around very long after the money tree drops its last leaf is pretty slim. In the phone room you can expect to hear the angry, disbelieving accusations and pleadings, plus the weeping, wailing, moaning, and gnashing of teeth when the recently devastated tycoons receive their pink slips from the land of *l'amour*.

It's really amazing to listen to some big, tough guy who is used to enforcing his will on those around him, particularly women, as he slowly absorbs the fact that he has been basically defanged and has virtually no leverage. Raising your voice and yelling into the phone doesn't get you very far when the person on the other end can cut you off completely by simply hanging up. Learning basic phone etiquette and phone skills is an extremely important acquisition for one's arsenal of good manners. Venting your anger and frustration on someone whom you think should be doing your bidding, looking after your interests, and on whom you are totally dependent doesn't wear very well.

It's crucial to realize that the loved ones your arrest has also "put in prison" are probably struggling with your absence and all the additional burdens they are now carrying as a result of it. If at all possible, always try to bring something to the conversation that adds to their sense of well-being and security. If the recipients of your phone communications begin to anticipate nothing more than a recitation of your grumblings and gripes, you can imagine how much they're going to look forward to hearing from you.

Be a good listener. You don't always have to respond or react immediately to something that's been said. Your special friend is going to want and need to vent anger and frustration, so be prepared. Even though it's not easy, be quiet and listen. Sometimes a person just needs to be heard. They don't necessarily need directions, solutions, or a list of "you should"s.

Phone courtesy at most camps asks that convicts limit their conversations to 15 minutes at a whack, hang up, and then get back in line if they wish to make another call. This level of respect for the needs of others is a beautiful thought, and that is generally as far as it goes. Phone traffic is highest after pay has been posted and people have money to spend. Every phone situation will have its own special rhythm, and each convict will have to figure out the optimal time to meet his personal needs. It wouldn't be a bad idea to call ahead to the camp you're being sent to and ask how its particular phone system works, as there are a wide variety of procedures existing within the BOP.

When you arrive at camp, you'll fill out a phone list with the names and numbers of those people you expect to be calling. The amount of people you are allowed to have on your list is determined at each camp, as are any additional regulations regarding phone communication. **It is against the rules to conduct business over the phone, and doing so**

can result in sanctions. This is another one of those randomly and arbitrarily enforced rules.

In the camp I was most recently in, it appeared that convicts were conducting business over the phone all the time, and not too cautiously. The ones who got hassled or into trouble over it were guys who spent literally hours a day conducting business, or had, through some other medium — such as the mail or the report of a snitch — brought their business activities to the attention of the authorities. Since all phone conversations at this particular camp were recorded (you should inquire as to your particular camp's policy), there was an aural record of everything that had been said, which made it impossible to deny engaging in certain types of unsanctioned activity. Once again, this is one of those areas where one has to decide if the profit-to-risk ratio is high enough. You would be well advised to question your convict comrades about the history of phone-related problems before engaging in any behavior you might later regret.

If you are in a camp where the Inmate Telephone System (ITS) is set up so you have phone credits, you are probably paying exorbitant rates which should shame even the most black-hearted capitalist. There are phone-forwarding businesses in existence which provide cheaper rates and the ability to place three-way calls, but once again, this is "frowned on" and can get you into a jam. Though tempting, this is another potential stumbling block to steer around.

As a general rule, the telephone is a benign presence in your life as a convict. Very often, it will be your most real and rewarding connection with life on the outside. How you interact with it will make you either light-hearted and better able to endure the rigors of prison-camp life, or morose and miserable as you live down your sentence. Take some time to think about what it might be like for the people on the other end, and how you can make your conversations a source of energy and empowerment. It will be time well spent.

Self-reliance is the premier quality that one should cultivate. That is extremely important. And another important tenet to adopt in terms of "surviving" federal prison camp, or any prison, for that matter, is an acceptance of these realities: you have no power, you will be forced to do many things that are objectionable, and you will be asked and told to participate in many things which will make no sense to you.

As a law-breaker, you have defied the system and challenged authority, and the powers-that-be have determined that you need to be shown who's boss. While in prison you will learn to do as you're told, and not ask questions. If someone tells you to mop a floor that has already been mopped five times that day and looks perfectly clean, just do it. When an officer gives you an order and his tone of voice is abusive or disrespectful, merely do what you're told and let it go at that. Situations such as these are excellent opportunities to practice self-control and anger management, and since you will have virtually no other recourse in moments of confrontation with both guards and convicts, you will be well-advised to adopt a non-reactive manner of response. Remember, should you get into a physical altercation with another convict in a federal prison camp, both the person who initiates the contact and the recipient go to the hole and get charged. People who are found guilty of physical violence typically get shipped out promptly to higher-security facilities.

Also, "non-attachment" to the outcome of events will help you get through the many inevitable moments of disappointment you will be faced with over the course of your imprisonment. For instance, if you go before your "team" (camp administrator, counselor, case manager) to request a furlough or some other privilege for which you have a reasonable expectation of receiving a favorable response, and you aren't overly concerned whether or not your request is granted, then if you are turned down for some capricious or inexplicable reason you won't be crushed. Guys with otherwise perfect records have been denied a furlough for something as inconsequential as leaving a piece of fruit out on their desk. Obviously, in a case like this, the administration has some hidden agenda, and no matter how great your need or how reasonable your explanation may be, they won't change their position. Always expect the unexpected.

It is impossible to overstate the need to refrain from hostilities. Some places where the potential for confrontations are greatest are the TV rooms and the dining hall. Generally speaking, there will be separate TV rooms for blacks, Hispanics, rednecks, and sports buffs. If you are someone who likes to watch the Arts & Entertainment channel, Public Broadcasting System, or anything that smacks of "Culture" with a capital "C," you might as well forget about watching TV while you're away, because the number of times you'll get your wish will be about as frequent as the appearance of Halley's comet.

After a few well-meant efforts to point out the enormously interesting program you have in mind to the totally hostile TV-room audience ("Honestly, dudes, the PBS special on the mating habits of the fuzz-billed ringwort is not to be missed!"), you'll cease your efforts and even stop thinking of your fellow viewers all as a "bunch of boring thugs." It's just the way it is. Moreover, if you don't give it up after the first serious wave of resistance, you're likely to be challenged by someone who would love to work off some aggression in front of an appreciative and "see no evil" group who has just enjoyed watching four hours of boxing reruns and would be thrilled to see you taken out in the first round. In all seriousness, the TV rooms are historically the location of the greatest number of spontaneous fights. Needless to say, the best thing to do when a programming disagreement comes up is capitulate.

After programming arguments, the next greatest source of strife is seating protocol. Nothing that happens in the TV rooms is worth risking expulsion from camp and relocation to a higher security-level facility, and your seat or lack thereof definitely isn't worth the gamble. The pecking order in the TV rooms usually has a hard core of TV junkies at the top. These are the guys who appear to open and close the place during prime viewing hours, have their own personal *TV Guides*, and whose life rhythms are dictated in large measure by the weekly viewing schedule.

Each TV-room subculture has its "ultimate leader" or "arbiter of taste." This person has been unofficially granted the right to select the shows and "channel surf" at will, as long as he retains the favor and approval of his TV room subordinates. Under the sway of the "alpha male" are the regulars who are either ethnically or culturally linked to him. These people usually keep chairs, with their cubicle numbers and names inscribed on the back, permanently located in the TV room, and, by virtue of this form of "squatting," feel they are entitled to enter the room and claim their seats at will. They also have more or less fixed positions in the room, and will take exception with someone who has moved their chairs.

To a newcomer or outsider, this can be an endless source of frustration. Don't be surprised to have someone come into the TV room and tell another convict to get up and move, even if the game's close, there's five minutes left to play, and the person being ordered about has been there from the very beginning of the broadcast. This is yet another opportunity to practice non-attachment and not allow your "problem with authority" button to be pressed.

The other major spawning ground for trouble is the dining hall. People tend to grumble and get testy when anything that interferes with the provision and consumption of their food occurs. Though not considered a particularly serious provocation, asking for specially served food ("extra potatoes, hold the rice, and no ham") while two hundred hungry, dissatisfied convicts are waiting behind you will generally elicit a few unfriendly comments. Many inmates, especially those who have come from higher-security prisons, are obsessively germ-conscious, and will become downright belligerent if you make the mistake of reaching across their food trays while attempting to snag a food item or utensil lying in their trays' paths. Though it's highly unlikely that anything more than a truly angry tongue-lashing would result from an oversight such as this in a prison camp, apparently many a convict has been shanked (knifed) in the higher-security prisons for such momentary behavioral lapses.

Finally, like everywhere else, cutting in line in order to get fed faster is not applauded. While nobody is apt to do anything to the line-cutter at the time of his infraction (especially if the offender is large and accompanied by his clique), this kind of untoward selfishness has its price, and doesn't go unnoticed. Remember: paybacks can be hell, and there are plenty of angry, frustrated convicts who have nothing better to do than obsess about your rude behavior and plot revenge.

Even though the "men's consciousness" movement has made it less of an uncool or unmanly thing to do, showing your emotions is still not really acceptable behavior in the prison system. Being emotional or sensitive will not serve you well, but if you are that sort of person, you value these qualities and want to maintain them, so that when you are ultimately released you will continue to exhibit this "added dimension" of your personality. Limited physical contact and emotional intimacy with your loved ones, a physically sterile environment, and overall sensory deprivation will take a toll on even the strongest psyche, so keep this in mind. It's vitally important to do things that nurture this loving, open part of your personality. The less you exercise your heart-based emotional attributes, the more atrophied these skills will become, and the longer your post-release recovery time will be. Because you have so much less to work with while in prison, you'll have to tap into areas and abilities (letter writing, expressing caring in non-physical ways, etc.) that are either little-used or totally alien to you. The question is not whether or not you'll physically survive federal prison camp, but how damaged you'll be when you are released.

Because there is so much pain involved throughout the entire penal process — arrest, pre-trial, adjudication, incarceration, return to civilian life — one's natural response to the whole thing is to contract and, in a sense, assume a sort of mental fetal position, hoping that by doing so one can avoid a fatal jab from one's tormentors. However, at some point after regaining your balance, the process of restoring and expanding mental and spiritual health must begin, and this can only be done when your eyes are open and carefully trained on the task ahead.

After you begin to get oriented in your new "life" setting, find a job, and get some sense of what your schedule will be like, it's important to figure out what you want to get out of the prison-camp experience and how you're going to go about accomplishing it. Goal-setting and discipline will lend structure and focus to what is paradoxically both a highly structured and chaotic experience. If you choose to devise a schedule that permits a lot of free time — orderly jobs fall into this category — you can create an environment that closely resembles a somewhat restrictive college campus or a monastic order. On the other hand, if you want to be in a situation where you don't have to think too much and can just do what you're told to do, there is ample opportunity for this scenario.

To a great extent, the prison-camp experience is how you choose to perceive it. You can run around complaining, and accentuate the negative, or you can view this time as an opportunity to do some productive things for yourself and your family that you would otherwise never be able to do. The Chinese belief that there is "opportunity in crisis" is very true. You simply have to be willing to take advantage of the situation when it arises. This is another occasion to "eat bitter" (more Chinese wisdom) and grow strong from it.

In an atmosphere that naturally lends itself to anger, resentment, and resistance, it is extremely important to overcome and tame these enemies of your well-being. The harder you fight and resist your circumstances, the more miserable you'll be. You cannot change the fact that the prison-camp personnel hold all the big guns and ammunition, and you will not "beat" them by challenging them in conventional ways. It's a bit like those "Chinese handcuffs" you played with as a child: the harder you pulled, the tighter they held your fingers.

If you view your life as a quest for knowledge and a journey of discovery, then it is possible to regard the incarceration experience as just part of a process, one instance on a long continuum of learning. Before you get to the castle where your reward awaits, you must first pass through a dark forest inhabited by demons and full of potentially life-threatening challenges. You must fend off the creatures which would devour you, and overcome the obstacles. Only then will you be worthy of the reward.

(There are several books that will be helpful to any person who is preparing to go to a federal prison camp. One is We're All Doing Time *by Bo Lozoff [Human Kindness Foundation, Durham, NC, 1985]. Another is* King Rat *by James Clavell [Delacorte Press, New York, 1983].)*

CHAPTER ONE
GUILTY

"What took you so long? The jury's in," your lawyers bark as they open the huge wooden door to the Federal courtroom. You walk into the room, as far as the low railing that divides spectators from participants. Your hands are shaking a little as you open the railing door, take three more steps, and then lower yourself gently into a chair at the defendant's table. The jury takes forever to enter the room. Only the third one from the right in the first row looks at you. Is that a bad sign? Or a good sign? You can't remember. Surely they didn't find you guilty, did they?

The foreman hands the bailiff a piece of paper. The bailiff gives the paper to the judge, and the judge reads it silently to himself. Does he seem surprised? Surprised at a not guilty verdict? Surprised at a guilty verdict? Why doesn't he just read it right now and get it over with? The whole proceeding seems to go in slow motion.

Then a voice from very far away says, "On the first count, guilty. On the second count, guilty." You hear a roar of noise. You look to your right, at the prosecution witnesses, bouncing up and down behind the Assistant U.S. Attorney. They are clapping and cheering. The judge bangs his gavel for silence. The Assistant U.S. Attorney twists her body around slowly and gives you a hateful and triumphant smile. Your lawyers walk over to shake her hand. "Oh, shit," you say to yourself as your eyes glaze over. "They found me guilty..."

In August of 1996, the Justice Department reported that the number of women and men in America's jails and prisons reached nearly 1.6 million last year. As of December 31, 1996, one out of every 167 Americans was in prison or jail. Just ten years earlier, only one out of 320 were in jail or prison. Simple math tells us that in another ten years, one out of approximately 80 Americans will be incarcerated some-where. Obviously, it won't be long before we'll all be in jail... or else working as guards or administrators.

In light of these depressing facts, here is some advice on how to survive a federal prison camp. In recent years, federal prison camps have become increasingly popular within the "justice" system for confining those convicts who are not considered to be high-risk and suitable for the more severe federal prisons. If you are one of those who have been sentenced to do time at a federal prison camp, this book is for you.

CHAPTER TWO
YOUR PSI OR
PRESENTENCING INTERVIEW

Immediately after the verdict is read, you will be taken to the Probation Department for a presentencing interview. This will result in your PSR, or Presentencing Report, which will become the most important document in your prison file. Prison officials will consider it to be their bible. They will use the information and the misinformation in your PSR to guide them in their treatment and mistreatment of you.

WHY THEY WANT
THE PRESENTENCING REPORT

In your Presentencing Report, the Probation Department recommends how much time you should have to serve, and what monetary restitution you should have to make for the crime of which you were just convicted. The PSR makes judgment calls about your motivation and your character. What you and others say in this interview will dog you for all of your career with Corrections. So beware, and be careful what you say. The person interviewing you is not your friend, and does not have your best interests at heart.

THEY MAY SPLIT YOU UP

The first thing that many probation officers will do is to call in your wife for a separate interview without you. The officer takes your spouse in first, because the officer hopes that she is angry with you now that you're guilty, and he hopes that she is bitter because of whatever you did or didn't do. The officer wants your wife to say terrible things about you so that the officer can write you a lousy Presentencing Report. Not all probation officers will use this tactic, but be prepared in case this happens.

LIES FROM OFFICERS

Remember this during the interview: the officer has been heavily trained in techniques to use to try to gain your confidence. This person knows that you are, emotionally, at one of the lowest points in your life. This person hopes that if he or she acts like the good cop, you will ruin your life a little bit more. So the probation officer will look at you with fake sincerity and say something like this: "Here is your chance to tell your side of the story."

Do not trust the probation officer for a moment. If there has been a trial (assuming that you didn't plead guilty and avoided one), you have already told your side to a jury of your peers in the courtroom. They didn't believe you, and this officer won't believe you either. This officer doesn't even want to believe you. What if the officer did believe you? Could the officer set you free? Would the officer even want to set you free? Not a chance in hell.

This is not the time to tell your side of the story. It is the time to "take responsibility for your crime and express remorse." If you do not do this, your Presentencing Report will say that you refuse to accept responsibility for your crime, and that you show no remorse for committing it. This is not good for you. Unfortunately, even when you DO show remorse, oftentimes your Presentencing Report will not take positive note of that fact. It will often be overlooked and not even mentioned. Many times, only bad things will be in your Presentencing Report. You can only hope that you are handled by a relatively fair-minded interviewer. Try to be as earnest and convincing as possible without laying it on too thick.

GET YOUR STORIES STRAIGHT

If both you and your wife are to be interviewed very quickly after trial or pleading, try to get your stories straight in advance. That's because at the Presentencing Interview, your wife may be asked questions, and then you both may be called in together. If this happens, you will not be given a chance to speak together privately. They want to catch the two of you telling different stories about your personal habits and behavior. Your wife may be asked questions like these:

What kind of person is your husband?
What kind of husband is he?
How would you describe him?
How would you describe your marriage?
How do your children feel about him?
Does he ever get violent with them?
Does he have any stepchildren?
How does he treat them?
Do they like him?
Do they get angry with him?

Why?
Does he ever get violent with you?
Has he ever done drugs? What kind? How often?
Does he drink alcohol? How often? How much?
What will you do now that he has been found guilty?
How will you support yourself?
Will you get a divorce?

At this point, your wife will probably feel very sad and very angry toward you. These feelings are normal and natural. But beware! It is very important for your spouse to control those angry feelings. Your wife should emphasize everything good about you: your good nature, your upbeat attitude, your cheerfulness, your heart of gold, your unselfishness, your generosity to relatives and friends, your patience, your sweet behavior to old folks, the great amount of time that you spend with the children, your kindness to animals. Your wife's goal should be to do and say everything necessary to get you back home as soon as possible. There will be plenty of private times for anger. This is NOT one of them.

THEY MAY CALL YOUR EX-WIFE

In his relentless search for derogatory information, the Pre-sentencing Report interviewer may contact your ex-wife or -wives, and as many as possible of her/their relatives, hoping that each of them still hate you for divorcing their perfect daughter(s). The interviewer may also try to speak privately to all of your ex-girlfriends, ex-business partners, any disgruntled customers, and your in-laws. Any teeny-tiny bad thing they say will go into your PSR as though it were the gospel truth. Unfortunately, if they say anything good about you, it will probably not be recorded in the Presentencing Report.

THEY WILL CALL YOUR LAST EMPLOYER

The Probation Officer will also call your "last employer." He or she wants to inform your last employer that you have been convicted of a crime in federal court. Then the Probation Officer will try to find out what bad things the employer has to say about you. Maybe it would embarrass you to have your former colleagues notified of your conviction. Maybe you think your old co-workers would love to say bad things about you. Or maybe you just don't think it's any of their damn business. In order to avoid these possibilities, get yourself a job at a fast-food restaurant right before your trial. That fast-food restaurant will then become your "last job." Then the probation folks can call your "last employer" to their heart's content, and it won't matter at all.

DEFENDANT'S OBJECTIONS
TO THE PRESENTENCING REPORT

You do have an opportunity to object to the Presentencing Report and the conclusions it draws. Since the PSR has a major impact on sentencing guideline requirements, of course you will hope that your objections will help. However, do not expect any of your objections, even if true, to have any effect whatsoever upon the PSR. The PSR is prepared by the Probation Department and your objections to it are reviewed by the Probation Department. What do they care if you object? In most instances, they are unlikely to change the conclusions they have already drawn. Still, it doesn't hurt to submit a well-written and reasonable account of your objections, just in case somebody, somewhere, cares about your case.

GET IT IN WRITING FROM THE JUDGE

At your sentencing hearing, the judge will rely heavily upon the recommendations in your PSR. Occasionally, the judge will mumble something such as, "I did not take into account the negative remarks your ex-wife made about you, so don't worry about it." If the judge says something like this, make sure he or she instructs the Probation Office to remove the ex-wife's remarks from your PSR. Follow up to be sure that this is done. Otherwise, when you get to the federal prison camp, the officials there will believe what your ex-wife said was true. After all, it is right there in black and white in your PSR. They will penalize you for her spiteful and untruthful remarks because the prison officials rely on "the bible" when they deal with you.

CHAPTER THREE
GET YOUR LIFE IN ORDER

If there is even a remote chance you will be sentenced to prison, now is the time to get your life in order. Pretend that you will be abducted by aliens, and ask yourself what you can do to make life easier for your wife, your children, your parents, and so on, while you are out of the galaxy.

A GOOD WAY TO SELL YOUR BUSINESS

If you haven't sold your business yet, and you think that it would be a good idea to do so, contact your competitors right away. Call the three best ones and schedule a private meeting with each. You want to sell your business for as much down payment as possible and as short a payment period as possible. If the proposals seem somewhat equal, go with the offer that gives you the biggest down payment. Then if the buyer decides to screw you and not make all of his payments because you are in prison, at least you have gotten a large down payment.

SELLING YOUR PERSONAL ASSETS

It may be that you will be forced to liquidate your assets because of the interruption in your income. If this is so, sell your house. When you go to jail there will be only one income. Most inmates' wives end up losing their family homes because they cannot keep up the payments by themselves. There is no point in losing the equity in your home due to foreclosure. Usually you have about four months between your guilty verdict and your date to report for your jail sentence. So sell your house while you still have some time, and can be present to oversee the transaction.

You may want to sell everything you can. If you have two cars, you should probably sell one. Then your wife will only have to buy insurance for one.

Some convicts want to convert all of their assets to cash so their families can move closer to where they are serving their time. You should seriously consider whether or not this is a reasonable course of action. True, having your family in close proximity means that weekend visiting is more convenient. But virtually all federal prison camps are in rural, economically depressed areas, near small towns that offer few, if any, opportunities for employment other than the nearby prison and/or prison camp. And there are no conjugal visits allowed in federal prison camps. So these factors must be taken into account before the decision to move one's family near the federal prison camp is made.

If your family decides to move closer, then you may decide to sell most, if not all, of your material goods, and get cash now!

MAKE SURE YOUR WIFE HAS A JOB

A high-paying job is best, of course. But if that is not possible, a transferable job is good, too. Sales, nursing, retail, and travel industry jobs generally are transferable to wherever you go, if your family decides to make such a move.

CHAPTER FOUR
FINDING OUT ABOUT SPECIFIC
FEDERAL PRISON CAMPS

EVERY PRISON CAMP IS DIFFERENT

Every prison camp is different. There are over 66 institutions in the federal prison system. There are stories that FPC Allentown in Pennsylvania, and FPC Eglin in Florida are the easiest in the prison system. "Country-club prisons" is what they are called. However, many of the camps' reputations are based upon rumors from inmates at other camps. For example, at most prison camps, the inmates hear rumors that the prison camp at Tyndall Air Force Base is wonderful. They hear that visits are unsupervised in a park-like atmosphere. They hear tales of happy families with big picnic baskets stuffed full of food and treats for visiting days. I doubt these rumors are true, but the inmates are all hopeful, and at the times when they are depressed, they are more willing to suspend disbelief.

DON'T GO TO A CAMP THAT IS ATTACHED TO A HIGH-SECURITY PRISON

You want to be sent to a prison camp that is NOT attached to a heavy-duty prison. Prisons are classified from low-security level camps for white collar and drug-related offenders, up through high-security prisons for violent and dangerous offenders. Pete Rose went to a low-level prison camp that was attached to a maximum-security prison located near Marion, Illinois. The problem with a camp attached to a high-level prison is that a prison camp is basically a work camp. You will be assigned a job to perform every day. Most of the inmates in an attached low-security prison camp are given jobs inside the walls of the heavy-duty, high-security prison. There is a certain amount of danger involved. And the guards at such an attached camp like to threaten that they'll send you to the higher-level prison if you don't behave, or follow their orders, or whatever.

ASK FOR A CAMP ON A MILITARY BASE

Here is what you want: You want to go to a prison on a military base. The military asks for these prison camps so the inmates will do the work that the military does not want to do. Some of this work includes cutting grass, running errands, light typing, cleaning bathrooms, and any other repetitious or dirty job that the military does not care to perform.

ASK FOR REFERENCES

Each camp on a military base is different, of course. And there are always inmate rumors about each one. To find out the truth, speak with people who have actually been in a specific camp recently. Ask your lawyer for referrals. Your lawyer may have some former clients who are being released from federal prison camp, or may be able to refer you to an attorney who does. For starters, ask about federal prison camps at Tyndall Air Force Base, at Eglin Air Force Base, and at Saufley Field Naval Facility. They are in Florida and have good reputations.

HOW TO REQUEST THE PRISON CAMP THAT'S BEST FOR YOU

Requests for specific prison camps are usually granted if they are close to your loving and supportive family members. If you want to be close to your parents, mention that they are loving and supportive, and ask for a prison near their permanent home.

If your parents are not particularly supportive, or if you and your wife and kids want to be somewhere else, you need to get a residence there before you are sentenced. The judge will get pissed if he thinks that you're just camping out in a certain locale in order to get a better prison location. If your family decides to relocate to be near you, move them to where you want to be, and be sure that they are "settled" with schools and jobs. Then request a prison camp near your loving and supportive wife and children. But be sure that what you're planning to do is best for your family, and not just an ego trip designed to make you feel more in control of your destiny.

WHAT TO EXPECT AT YOUR SENTENCING HEARING

You need to remember that the judge in your case does not give a rat's butt about you. Your judge can cancel your sentencing hearing at any time before your sentencing date. Call to confirm the sentence date so you don't make a long trip for nothing.

At your sentencing hearing, the judge will do whatever the PSR says to do. Most PSRs recommend a sentence range, and most judges will give you a sentence right in the middle. If your recommended sentence range is 30 to 36 months, your judge will probably sentence you to 33 months in prison.

At this hearing, the judge has the choice to either take you into custody right then, or to let you self-surrender at the institution. It is very important to self-surrender. If you self-surrender, the judge believes you to be a low risk. When you get to prison, your security rating will be lower. This is good.

DIESEL THERAPY

If you don't self-surrender, you will be taken away in handcuffs and placed in the local jail. You end up staying there for two or three months, and then you get what is known as diesel therapy. Diesel therapy means you are bussed around from town to town until you get to your prison. The bus is called the Silver Bullet. Other prisoners will be picked up and dropped off along the way. At night you will be staying in local jails wherever you are. While you are in the Silver Bullet, you are shackled at the ankles and wrists. This makes relieving yourself very difficult, because you cannot get to your zipper or the toilet paper. The worst inmates have to wear special handcuffs, and they are always asking someone nearby to push the handcuffs back up because they hurt. The Silver Bullet itself is comfortable. But several officers with shotguns are riding along with you to keep order. The whole scenario will remind you of the movie *The Fugitive*.

PLANNING AFTER YOUR SENTENCING

At your sentencing hearing, the judge does not tell you where you are going to jail to serve your time. The judge can only say "I recommend" this or that jail if there is room. It is up to the BOP to assign you a space. So don't get your hopes up too high at your sentencing hearing if your judge recommends the prison camp that you want. The prison officials can disagree. And in the end, you have to report wherever they tell you to go.

What you do know after your sentencing hearing is the exact date when you will be leaving the free life. You will discover that you have approximately two months left before your "report date," the day when you must report to jail. Ten days before your report date, you'll be served with an Order to Surrender that shows your reporting date and time and an actual prison-camp location. Before your Order to Surrender, you will not know where you will be sent. Your family may accompany you when you report if you wish.

During this period, your life is under even more stress. After being indicted and before going to prison, some inmates gain between 40 and 100 pounds of weight. You may gain this much yourself. Eat and drink, and be as merry as you can. Do not feel guilty about it. Guilt will add more stress. You will have plenty of time to get back into shape once you get to prison, if that's what you want to do.

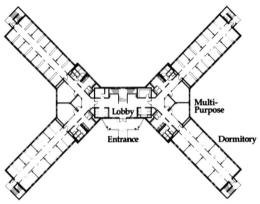

Satellite Camp Housing

The 250 minimum-custody inmates of the Satellite Camp are housed in two, two-story buildings. Living quarters feature dormitory cubicles in each of the four building wings. Multi-purpose and counseling rooms, toilet/shower rooms, are grouped at the center of the building.

Concentrate as much energy as you can on getting all of your personal and financial affairs in order, and, if you decide to do so, converting all of your remaining assets to cash.

If there are only two or three prison-camp sites nearby, go visit the areas. Look for housing for your family, in case they decide to relocate near you. Look at the school systems. Check for nice neighborhoods. The rents should be reasonable because most of the prisons are in rural and/or economically depressed areas. Fill out credit applications at places that you would consider renting, but don't put any money down until you've gotten your Order To Surrender, telling you exactly where you'll be, and have finalized your post-incarceration plans.

SEE YOUR DOCTORS ABOUT YOUR PHYSICAL CONDITION

Schedule appointments with your doctors. If you are taking any medications, you need to get a letter from your physician stating what medication you require. Many inmates are on medication for high blood pressure or diabetes, for example. This letter from your doctor will enable you to bring your own medication into the camp. Otherwise you will have to wait for sick call to get new medications.

DON'T FORGET YOUR OLD INJURIES AND PHYSICAL LIMITATIONS

Have your doctor re-examine your physical condition. Do you have any old injuries from sports or accidents? Do you have a bad back or weak ankles? Would they be aggravated if you were assigned a physically demanding job? Here are some of the things that your doctor should document for you:

- bad back. Maybe you can't lift over 10 pounds. Maybe you require a bedboard for good rest.
- neck or whiplash problems. Maybe you can't lift over 10 pounds. Maybe you need two pillows to sleep properly.
- knee problems. Maybe you can't lift or carry over 10 pounds.
- foot problems. Maybe you need a soft-shoe permit, so you can wear sneakers on the job.
- overweight. Maybe you will need "chronic care" and have to check in once a month with the doctor. This means that you must lose one-half to a whole day of work each month.
- sleepwalker. You will need to sleep in the most desirable lower bunk.

GET THE DOCTOR TO PUT IT IN WRITING

Your doctor must document this information for you. Discuss your prior injuries with your doctor. Do you need special shoes for foot problems? The physician must document it for you. If your doctor feels that you cannot lift more than 10 pounds due to some injury that you may have had, you need to have the doctor put that in writing. This written doctor's report will give you a medical reason why you can't do any heavy physical labor such as running a weed eater for eight hours a day. It may help you get a bedboard or a bottom bunk. It will not mean that you cannot participate in camp sports.

GET YOUR TEETH CLEANED AND REPAIRED

See your dentist and have your teeth cleaned. It is very difficult to get a dentist to clean your teeth when you are in prison. The dentists prefer to postpone cleaning your teeth until the month preceding your release from prison. Have any dental problems such as cavities corrected now. Most prison dentists would rather pull out all of your teeth than repair them. You could emerge toothless at the end of your sentence.

CHAPTER FIVE
WHAT TO BRING WHEN YOU
REPORT TO PRISON CAMP

There are several things to be sure to bring with you when you actually report to serve your sentence at a federal prison camp.

BRING YOUR RECEIPT FOR YOUR FINE

Be sure to bring the receipt for the fine you were ordered pay at sentencing. You will need this receipt to prove that you actually paid your fine. If you could not pay your fine at sentencing, the prison will deduct $25 per quarter towards payment. The same $25 will be deducted whether you owe $200 or $200 million.

BRING PERSONAL CLOTHING

To find out what you can bring in the personal-clothing category, you need to call the institution after you receive your Order to Surrender. They will send you a list of what you can bring with you. This list is preliminary, because it changes from day to day. Note: Some federal prison camps do not allow any red or blue clothing, because those are colors commonly associated with the Bloods and Crips gangs. Find out whether or not this policy is in effect at the federal prison camp you are slated to enter. It would be wise not to bring any clothing of either of these colors in, just to be on the safe side.

DO NOT BRING EXTRAS OF EVERYTHING

Some convicts erroneously bring two or three times the amount of items that are allowed, hoping that they will encounter a lax administration that will allow them to bring extra items in. This is not a good idea. The object of every prison-camp resident should be to remain as inconspicuous as possible. By bringing in extra items, you are taking a chance that you may be stopped from bringing these extra items in. If that happens, the guards will have to do the one thing they hate most: work. They will have to count up the extra items, make note of them, and either store them until your release or (more likely) ship them home for you prepaid. In either case, you will have caused them some extra work, and they will take note of you and remember your name. So don't take the chance, and follow the procedures carefully.

THEIR LIST CHANGES FROM DAY TO DAY

Even if you follow the list that they sent to you in advance, that list may change from day to day. Just bring everything on the list, and include a copy of the list. When you arrive for surrender, the administration may whip out a new and different list. Then they may take away some of the items you have brought with you. Those items will be boxed up and sent home prepaid. By keeping a copy of the list you were provided in advance, you minimize the aggravation that the work-leery guards may have towards you.

BRING THESE CLOTHES

Bring at least the following items in the personal clothing category (after checking to ensure that nothing contradicts the list you have been provided):

- ☐ 1 dress shirt with collar (for visits)
- ☐ 1 belt
- ☐ 1 sweater
- ☐ 1 jacket or wind breaker
- ☐ 1 pair jeans, dress pants or trousers (for visits). At Eglin Federal Prison Camp, you will not be allowed to wear gray pants for visits, because the guards wear gray pants, and they don't want to get themselves confused. Other prison camps have similar little rules.
- ☐ 1 pair of dress shoes/boots, (hard-soled, not tennis shoes)
- ☐ 6 white T-shirts
- ☐ 6 pairs of undershorts
- ☐ 1 sweatsuit
- ☐ 2 pairs of Bermuda shorts
- ☐ 1 pair of tennis shorts
- ☐ 2 pairs of good sneakers
- ☐ 1 pair of shower shoes (flip-flops or thongs)

No logos of any kind can be on any article of clothing. So if your sweatsuit or jacket has a logo on it, you need to have it removed. You can pay the people at alterations shops to remove logos for you. And remember: No blue or red clothing, excluding denim.

BRING TOILETRIES

Bring a lot of your own toiletries. The selection is a bit limited at the commissary.

- ☐ toothbrushes
- ☐ toothpaste
- ☐ razor and blades
- ☐ brush and combs
- ☐ hair gel containing no alcohol (No aerosol cans)
- ☐ fingernail clippers
- ☐ toenail clippers
- ☐ soap and soap container
- ☐ tweezers
- ☐ round point scissors
- ☐ shampoo
- ☐ deodorant (No aerosol cans)
- ☐ hand lotion (a good lubricating kind for personal moments with your private parts)
- ☐ shaving cream (No aerosol cans)

(There is no need to bring after-shave lotion or cologne. Who would you want to smell "good" for? You might attract the wrong sort of admirer.)

BRING MISCELLANEOUS ITEMS

Bring these things:

- ☐ wristwatch, valued at under $50 (Although you would be well advised to buy one at the commissary, just to make sure you don't wear anything flashy that could induce avarice in your fellow convicts.)
- ☐ up to 2 religious neckchains

☐ cheap, but reliable, pens and pencils
☐ sports equipment (weight belt, gloves, tennis racquet, tennis balls)
☐ Koran, Book of Mormon or other religious texts (There are plenty of bibles on hand.)
☐ all legal documents that you might need to help you file your appeals
☐ dictionary
☐ books to read (There are limits on the amount; check with your prison camp.)
☐ dentures
☐ eyeglasses
☐ contact lenses and cleaning solutions
☐ your personal address-and-telephone-number book
☐ medicines that you need (you'll need a doctor's letter)
☐ musical instrument and music books
☐ small, battery-powered night light

BRING YOUR SOCIAL SECURITY CARD

You will need your social security card, so that you can be properly exploited by the prison-industry scam.

DO NOT BRING PROHIBITED ITEMS

If it is not on their list, you can't bring it in. Don't bring anything that you know you can't have. There will be ways to get prohibited items, once you are actually in prison camp, but you'd be a fool to do so. If your urine analysis turns up positive, or you're written up for possessing a prohibited item, you'll be shipped out to a federal prison immediately. Don't try to bring anything that's prohibited in when you report, because you'll just make the guards mad at you.

DO NOT BRING CREDIT CARDS

There is nowhere to use them.

BRING A PHOTOCOPY OF YOUR DRIVER'S LICENSE

Do not bring your actual driver's license to prison. However, you should make a photocopy of your driver's license and bring that copy with you. That way, if you are required to drive as part of your assigned job, you might not have to take the written driver's test.

BRING MONEY WITH YOU

You are not allowed to have any paper money at all while you are in prison camp. However, you are allowed to spend about $100 per month during each month of your sentence (the amount varies from camp to camp). When you arrive for prison, the guards will take all of your money and give you a receipt. This money is deposited for you in your Trust Fund or your Commissary account. Then you can spend it as needed during your incarceration. Don't bring too much with you; $100 is an adequate amount.

EVEN IF YOU PAID YOUR FINE, DON'T BRING ALL YOUR ALLOWED MONEY WITH YOU

Some convicts bring $100 per month times all of the months of their sentence when they report. In other words, if they have a 24-month sentence, they bring $2,400 in cash. This is not a good idea. The guards will be not be happy about this, because you have so much money, and this is not good. In addition, it will make you a potential target for predators. It would be better to have a loved one or a bank send you $100 a month, which can be deposited to your commissary account.

WHAT IF YOU HAVE AN UNPAID FINE?

If you did not pay the fine imposed at sentencing, the prison will watch your commissary account carefully. If you have a lot of money in it, they will take that money and apply it toward your unpaid fine. You will not be allowed more than $10 extra per month. You need to find someone who has no money in his commissary account and pay him $10 per month, or so, to hold your money for you. Don't get overly trustful and deposit thousands or even hundreds of dollars into another convict's account at one time. Have a loved one or bank send him $100 or so every month. That way, if you get ripped off you can cut your losses.

WHY DO YOU NEED MONEY?

Prisons do not supply you with all of the things you need or want. You might want a deck of cards. You might want ice cream or cigarettes. You might require postage stamps, or stationery. You might yearn for a better grade of shampoo, or a couple of apples. You might desire a radio with earphones. You might want a wrist watch. You might need some "off the books" services.

FOR WHAT WILL YOU SPEND THE MOST?

Most of your money will be used to buy food. Food controls inmates. If you can buy your own food, you don't have to scam anyone out of it unless you want to. If you can buy your own food, you don't have to feel left out. There are very few things in prison to make you feel good. Food becomes a luxury item. Pamper yourself a little. If it makes you feel better to be able to buy yourself some special foods when you want them, go ahead and do it.

MONEY FOR "OFF THE BOOKS" ITEMS

You will discover that one way for inmates to make money in prison is to work "off the books." This is strictly forbidden, of course. But unless you have extra money, you will be unable to pay for these "off the books" items. For example: Do you want a haircut? Haircuts are supposed to be free in prison. In real life, you will have to pay another inmate for your haircuts, and the price is usually $2 to $5. Do you want an inmate lawyer to help you with some legal problems? If you do, you will have to pay the inmate lawyer whatever he charges you for this service. Do you want a bit of extra food from the food service workers? You will have to pay for it. Do you want someone to wash your clothes and make your bed? You have to pay, and it runs $50 to $75 per month.

SPECIAL HIGH-PRICED "OFF THE BOOKS" ITEMS

Some "off the books" services cost a lot more money. Settling large gambling debts in prison requires an elaborate repayment plan. In this plan, your relative on the outside (your wife, or maybe your brother) sends money to the inmate's relatives on the outside. Gambling is a HUGE industry within the prison walls, perhaps partially due to boredom. If you are a skilled gambler, you can make good money. Of course, if you are not a skilled gambler, you can lose good money. You are better off if you do not gamble. Not only do you run the risk of losing, but it is against prison rules, and can get you shipped out. If you gamble and lose, do not fail to pay up promptly. The life you save may be your own.

WHAT YOU WILL BE GIVEN TO WEAR

You will be issued government clothing to wear. It varies, but here is what is issued at a typical prison camp:

- ☐ 4 blue shirts
- ☐ 4 blue trousers
- ☐ 4 undershorts
- ☐ 4 white t-shirts
- ☐ 1 belt
- ☐ 1 handkerchief
- ☐ 1 raincoat
- ☐ 1 pair safety shoes
- ☐ 1 set bedsheets
- ☐ 1 pillowcase
- ☐ 1 pillow
- ☐ 2 blankets
- ☐ 3 pair white socks (Note: These socks will be acrylic, and they suck! Be sure to bring in cotton socks. As a matter of fact, nearly all BOP-issued clothing is made of synthetic materials. If you are allergic to such materials, or have strong feelings against them, too bad! You'll have to bring in your own, or make do with what you are issued.)
- ☐ 2 towels
- ☐ 1 washcloth

In winter you may be issued:

- ☐ 1 sweatshirt

☐ 1 set thermal underwear
☐ 1 blue jacket
☐ 1 navy watchcap

(Note: Not all prison camps issue winter clothing.)

If you need to exchange or replace damaged clothing at the clothing room, you use an "Inmate Request To Staff Member," commonly called a "cop-out."

CHAPTER SIX
YOUR FIRST DAY

HOW YOU GET TO PRISON

There are several ways to transport yourself to the prison itself. You can arrive by cab from the airport or from the bus station. You can arrive on the Silver Bullet. Or your family can bring you to the prison camp.

But even if your family drives you to the prison gates, only you can walk through the front door. You know that you are crazy for doing this, but you open up the door and self-surrender to prison.

HOW YOU ACTUALLY SURRENDER

You enter the door to the federal prison camp. You are in a lobby area. There will probably be one or two other inmates reporting at the same time. You will actually feel better knowing that you are not the only one going through this nightmare. You will be taken to another room where they will go through all your belongings and tell you what you can keep and what you can't keep. You will give them the money that you brought for deposit to your commissary account, and they will give you a receipt for it.

THEY ASSIGN YOU A NUMBER

The hacks assign you an inmate number. It is a six-digit number followed by three more numbers. The last three numbers represent the location where you were convicted of your crime. The first six may be meaningless.

DON'T CALL THEM "HACKS," "SCREWS," OR "SNOUTS" TO THEIR FACES

Although guards are routinely referred to as "hacks," "screws," "snouts," and lots of other terms of non-endearment, do not call any prison official a "hack" or any other euphemism to his face, unless you are anxious to get shipped out.

THEY STRIP-SEARCH YOU

Most camps strip-search you. These strip searches can and will include body-cavity searches, including your asshole. That's when you know you've arrived.

THEY MAKE YOU ANSWER QUESTIONS

The hacks will tell you to fill out a questionnaire about some basic medical issues. Be sure to report if you are a sleepwalker, so you can get a lower bunk. Usually you only get the lower bunk on a seniority basis unless you have a medical excuse. Walking in your sleep is an important medical excuse.

YOU STEP INTO FEDERAL PRISON CAMP

Soon you push through another door into the prison itself. It's a bit terrifying. But the reality is not as bad as you've imagined it. Nobody jumps you. Nobody rapes you. Nobody punches you or tries to kill you with a homemade knife. Everyone stares at you and checks you out. The hack takes you to your bunk.

YOU GET YOUR CLOTHING

When you first arrive, the hacks give you a slip of paper so you can get your prison attire. Next, you go to the laundry room to collect that clothing. Inmates working in the laundry room issue your clothes to you, and they put your name and inmate number on the various articles of clothing. You go back to your bunk and put away all of your gear. You are now free to roam around.

YOUR FIRST NIGHT IN PRISON

On your first evening, you might want to go up to the visiting room. Usually there are several groups of people playing spades, bridge, hearts, and dominoes. By this time, it's pretty obvious that you are not going to be raped or physically assaulted. Just play it cool and don't intrude on anyone's conversation or activities. Don't be a loudmouth or a wiseass. Don't impose on anybody. You'll soon meet other convicts, and it won't be long before you'll be saddled with the burden of communication, which means that you'll spend more time than you'd like listening to the ramblings and stream-of-consciousness musings of people whom you would ordinarily never spend any time talking with in the outside world.

A & O

When you first arrive at federal prison camp, you are assigned to Admission and Orientation, known as A & O. Some convicts refer to you as a "fish" at this stage, and call your living quarters "the fish tank." You will remain there every day for two to three weeks. During this time, you will be given lectures by the warden and by personnel from all prison departments. Also on the agenda are physical examinations, interviews by staff members, intelligence tests, and psychological tests. Theoretically, this is to assist the Classification Team to get you a permanent job assignment. In practicality, it is to find out how you fit into the prison camp hierarchy, and decide what to do with you.

WILL YOU BE RAPED IN PRISON CAMP?

When you report to camp for the first time, the biggest question in your mind is, "Am I going to be raped like I've seen on TV?"

The answer is NO. Violence is generally NOT tolerated at a Level 1 prison. If you are caught fighting, hitting, punching, or in any other physical contact, you are shipped out of the camp. Prisoners caught fighting are shipped to a higher-level prison, and no one wants to go to a higher-level prison. Being shipped to a higher-level prison is called "going down further." Being in prison is called "being down." "I've been down for six months," means "I've been in prison for six months."

That is not to say that violence doesn't ever happen at a Level 1 camp. But it is the exception rather than the rule because at this level, if you are involved in a fight, you will be snitched out by the other inmates and then shipped by the hacks. Many of your fellow convicts are at the federal prison camp because they snitched off someone "up the ladder" from themselves in order to get a sentencing break. Everyone in the federal prison system knows this, so it should come as no surprise that there are plenty of people who are ready, willing, and able to snitch you off in order to curry favor with the administration. Many convicts at higher-level security prisons have nothing but contempt for those who are confined in the federal prison camps.

Keep in mind that violence can and will erupt at any time, and over the slightest provocation. It happens less frequently in the prison camps, but the motivating factors are always present: fear, anger, resentment, boredom, and stupidity. Be on your toes, and keep to yourself as much as possible until you learn the ropes.

SOME DO'S AND DON'TS

Don't borrow or accept anything from anyone. Don't offer to lend anyone anything. Other convicts will sometimes try to put you in their debt by loaning you cigarettes or other items on credit. This is called "lending you up," and can lead to very unpleasant repercussions. Be as self-sufficient as possible, and don't shoot off your mouth.

When someone asks you what you are in for, tell them the bare facts, but don't elaborate. When they ask you how long you are in for, tell them what your "top" time is. Again, don't elaborate.

EVERYONE IS A POTENTIAL SNITCH

At a high-level prison, snitches are in grave danger. They can be killed. But that's not as likely to happen at a low-level prison. An inmate snitch at a low-level prison receives a lot of real benefits by reporting any violation of the rules to the hacks. If you are a snitch at a low-level prison, the hacks will look the other way if you screw up. You can smuggle easier, and you can get sex visits easier. Consequently, at this level of prison, you have to assume that EVERYBODY is a snitch.

Still, snitches are constantly in danger. There are some convicts in the low-level prisons who have gotten there after doing a substantial amount of time at higher-level prisons. They have absorbed the contempt and hatred for snitches that forms the backbone of the convicted-class ethic, and are not apt to be understanding of those weak-willed convicts who try to feather their own stool-pigeon nests by informing on their fellow convicts. Consequently, the life of a snitch is often fraught with peril, and since no one trusts him, not even the hacks, he in turn can trust no one at all. Everyone despises a snitch, even those who use his services.

Don't be a snitch.

CHAPTER SEVEN
SCHEDULES, RULES AND JOBS

YOUR OFFICIAL DAILY SCHEDULE

Everything in federal prison camp runs on a schedule. Here is a typical daily schedule at a federal prison camp from Monday through Friday:

5:30 a.m.:	Lights On and Showers Open
5:30 – 6:30 a.m.:	Breakfast
6:00 – 8:15 a.m.:	Sick Calls
6:30 –7:00 a.m.:	Work Call
6:45 a.m.:	Showers Closed for Cleaning. After cleaning, they are opened again.
10:30 a.m.:	Lunch for Camp Details
11:00 a.m.:	Lunch for Base Details
11:00 a.m. – 12:00 noon:	Commissary Inquiries
11:30 a.m.:	Work Call for Camp Details

How To Survive Federal Prison Camp

12:00 noon:	Work Call for Base Details

Islamic Jumah Prayer Services on Friday

2:00 – 3:00 p.m.:	Commissary Open except Wednesday
4:30 – 8:15 p.m.:	Commissary Re-Opens
2:00 p.m.:	Check-Off for Dorm Orderlies, A&O, Base Details
2:00 p.m. – 3:45 p.m.:	Stamp and Coin Sales in Commissary on Wednesday Only
2:30 p.m.:	Mail Pick-Up by Dorm Officer
2:30 – 3:45 p.m.:	Clothing Exchange
3:00 p.m.:	Work Day Ends
8:00 a.m. – 3:45 p.m.:	Telephones On

After 4:00 count clears, the phones will be turned back on until 9:45 p.m.

3:00 – 3:30 p.m.:	Mail Room Open House (Tuesday-Friday)

R & D Open House (Tuesday–Friday)

3:00 – 3:45 p.m.:	Record Office Open House (Wednesday & Friday)
3:30 p.m.:	Recall in Preparation for Count and Mail Call
3:45 p.m.:	Mail Call in Dormitories

4:00 p.m.:	Official Count. Stand-up Bedside Count. This is the most important count of the day.
4:00 p.m.:	After count clears, Evening meal for one hour.
4:30 – 6:00 p.m.:	Stamp and Coin Sales Wednesdays
6:30 p.m. – 7:30 p.m.:	Special Commissary Purchases (Wednesday)
8:00 p.m. – 9:30 p.m.:	Jewish Religious Services, Friday only
10:00 p.m.:	Recall in Preparation for Count
10:10 p.m.:	Official Count
10:30 p.m.:	In Dormitories except for TV viewing, quiet room only until completion of 11:00 movie
10:30 p.m.:	Lights Out
11:00 p.m. – 5:30 a.m.:	Showers Closed

SCHEDULE FOR SATURDAYS, SUNDAYS, AND HOLIDAYS

On Saturdays, Sundays, and Holidays, the schedule is a bit different.

6:30 a.m.:	Showers Open
6:30 a.m. – 7:15 a.m.:	Continental Breakfast

8:00 a.m. – 9:45 p.m.:	Telephones Open
8:00 a.m.:	A&O Check-Off
8:00 a.m. – 3:30 p.m.:	Visiting Hours
8:30 a.m. – 10:30 a.m.:	Brunch
8:45 a.m.:	Protestant Services on Sunday
10:00 a.m.:	Catholic Services on Saturday
11:45 a.m.:	Cut–off for inmates being called to visiting room in preparation for Count
12:15 p.m.:	Recall in Preparation for Count
12:30 p.m.:	Official Count
1:00 p.m.:	Islamic Religious Services on Sunday
2:30 p.m.:	A & O Check-Off
3:45 p.m.:	Recall in Preparation for Count
4:00 p.m.:	Official Count, Standup Bedside Count

After count clears, one hour for Evening Meal

9:45 p.m.:	Recall in Preparation for Count
10:00 p.m.:	Official Count
10:30:	Lights Out
11:00 p.m. – 6:30 a.m.:	Showers Closed

CUBICLE RULES

Each inmate lives in a cubicle known as his "house" or "cube." Some prison camps do not allow TV sets in the cubicles. In those that do, TV sets are left on until the stations go off the air each night. You can visit cubicles in your dorm only, and only until 10:00 p.m.

ASSIGNMENT TO PERMANENT WORK

After your A&O, you will be assigned to a permanent work detail by the Classification Team. Theoretically, these are based upon institutional needs and upon your physical condition, aptitude, educational level, and previous working experiences. Actually, job assignments are generally assigned at random unless you have a friend already working in an area, and that friend asks for you by name.

GOOD JOBS AND BAD JOBS... AND WHY

During your first two weeks, every inmate will give you advice about what is the best job in the camp. No two inmates will tell the same story.

There are two types of jobs, based upon the location of the work. On one type of job, you stay inside the prison camp for the whole day. On the other type of job, you go outside of the prison camp to work on the military base itself. At some camps, most of the inmates want to get jobs within the prison camp. At other camps, most of the inmates want to get jobs out on the military base. Of course, there are advantages and disadvantages to both. The advantages of staying in the camp are that you will not have very much work to do, and you will have more access to the recreational items that you like, such as reading books or lifting weights. If you go on base (outside of camp), the advantages are street food, the ability to look at people other than inmates, and less hassle from the hacks.

IN CAMP YOU WON'T HAVE MUCH WORK TO DO

Jobs in the prison camp are not very time-consuming. You might be told to rake the leaves in a 100-square-foot area. You might have to clean toilets in one restroom. Most of your time will be spent hiding from the hacks so they won't know you're not working. Just do your job right, and you won't get written up or shipped out.

IN CAMP YOU CAN WORK OUT OR READ BOOKS

During times when you are not working, you can lift weights, read books, watch TV, write letters, study, or work "off the books" to earn extra money. There will be a lot of time when you are not working.

ON BASE YOU GET STREET FOOD

Street food is an important benefit you get when you work on-base rather than in the prison camp. You are allowed to take $1 a day with you when you leave the camp for your job. Most inmates save up that money, and if their boss is a decent sort of person, when they have enough money saved they will be allowed to order pizza or some other food they all agree upon.

ON BASE YOU CAN SEE PEOPLE WHO ARE NOT CONVICTS

The opportunity to look at people who aren't prison inmates is very important to most people. It helps to prevent the sort of paranoia that many prisoners experience after a while. Looking at the women on base helps your sexual fantasies, too. After nothing but looking at magazines, it's nice to see the real thing.

ON BASE THERE IS LESS HASSLE FROM THE HACKS

Being out of the prison camp means that you get less hassle from the hacks. It's the same old story: "Out of sight, out of mind." The more time you spend away from the hacks, the less time those hacks have to develop a bad attitude towards you. This means a lot less heartache for you.

THINGS NOT TO DO ON BASE

Some convicts think that working on base provides a good opportunity to smuggle items into the prison and perhaps arrange for sex visits with your wife. True, these opportunities exist. It is oftentimes possible to smuggle items into the prison camp by placing the contraband in the small of your back, or perhaps taping it on your inner thigh where many hacks will not pat-search you. But this is a stupid idea, and for more than one reason.

If you do get caught, you will immediately get shipped out to a higher-level prison. And if you get away with your smuggling endeavor, you will open yourself to being snitched on by those convicts who are always yearning to inform on somebody.

As far as sex visits go, your wife or a willing female sex partner is usually able to drive onto the military base just like any other visitor. Several colleges have branches on military bases, and a woman can state that she wants to attend. She can get a library card at the base library, and can come in to borrow or return books. During those times she is on base, it is possible to rendezvous in her car or elsewhere and have sex.

This is another stupid idea, because the authorities are on the lookout for it. If you get caught, off you go to a higher-level prison. The risk is not worth it.

The *Miami Herald* reported on May 18, 1996, that an Army sergeant was going to be court-martialed for allowing inmates at Eglin Federal Prison Camp to visit wives and girlfriends. He was accused of accepting bribes in exchange for allowing unsupervised visits with inmates who did yard work and other maintenance on the military base.

This is not uncommon. Each year, inmates who work on the military bases actually get their wives pregnant during their jail time! But, if you are truly concerned about surviving federal prison camp and getting released in the shortest possible time, you will bypass the so-called "opportunity for sex visits," and not take the chance of getting caught with your pants down.

SPECIFIC DETAILS ABOUT PRISON CAMP JOBS

Food Service: Cooks, bakers, salad men, orderlies, dishwasher operators, and clerks. These jobs give you a lot of power. They offer excellent possibilities to get shipped out, because you will be able to smuggle food out of the kitchen and sell it to other inmates if you so desire, thus placing yourself at the mercy of snitches. The access to food will help you to make "friends" easily. And food service workers get the best food.

Mechanical Services: Electricians, roofers, plumbers, cement finishers, mechanics, welders, masons, carpenters, painters, motor repairmen, clerks, and laborers. These jobs are hard work, and there is not much chance for you to earn extra income.

Business Office: Clerks. These inmates generally make more money ($100 per month), but there is not much chance for you to earn extra income.

Camp Hospital: Orderlies, clerks, technical assistants. These jobs are easy and indoors. However, there is no chance for you to earn extra income.

Education: Teacher aides, librarians, clerks. These jobs are easy and indoors. However, there is no chance for extra income for you.

Clothing Room: Clothing dispensers, clerks. These are excellent jobs. They are easy. They are indoors. You will have access to bleach, which you can sell to others, if you want to risk getting snitched off and shipped out. They offer many possibilities for "off the books" income for convicts who wish to be snitched off and shipped out. You can wash people's clothing. You can give them new clothes. You can give them extra clothes. All these services can be worth a lot of money to you, if you're stupid enough to value profiteering over survival and the earliest possible release from a prison camp.

Camp Maintenance: Building orderlies, landscape workers. These jobs are not very good. They are outdoors, and they offer no way for you to make extra money.

Base Details: Laundry, motor pool, roads and grounds, warehouse equipment, warehouse maintenance, redistribution and marketing, power production, forestry, special services, commissary, shop VT, greenhouse, supply, base museum, mower shop, hospital, Judge Advocate's office. These are the jobs that are located outside the prison camp. They are on the military base. These are good jobs for the idiots who want to smuggle items into and out of the prison camp. They are also good if you want to chance getting caught porking your wife or girlfriend. You'll get better food, because you can buy it on base. And the scenery is better because you are out of prison and can see regular people. Commissary jobs are especially good for brainless fools who wish to steal inventory and sell it. Where would the snitches be without morons who set themselves up to be the victims of informants?

WORK EVALUATIONS

Your supervisor will prepare evaluations of your work performance every 30 to 90 days. These evaluations will come into play when you are being considered for participation in community activities, furloughs, and parole.

WHAT IF YOU HATE YOUR JOB?

You can change jobs. In general, they want to make you stay on a job six months before you are eligible to be considered for a job change. If you get a job and you don't like it, try to switch out as soon as possible. As with anything else in life, if you are persistent enough, you will generally get the job you want. But usually it takes at least 90 days.

YOUR PAY IS REAL LOW

Your pay will be from 11 cents to 38 cents per hour, and your pay will be deposited in your trust fund or commissary account on the first day of the month after the pay is earned.

COUNT

Each day, the guards count you and the other convicts at regular intervals. Count is taken 5 times a day, plus two extra counts on weekends and holidays. If you are in the visiting room during count, you leave your guests in the visiting room and go outside into the camp for count. Once the count is "cleared," you can resume your visit. If the count doesn't "clear," you remain outside until it does.

The most important count is the bedside count at 4:00 p.m. You stand beside your bed for this count. Usually all convicts are present, but once in a while, a convict will escape and be discovered missing at count.

WHAT YOUR LIVING AREA WILL LOOK LIKE

In a typical prison camp, your living cubicle will be approximately 8´ X 8´. On one side are the bunk beds. On the opposite side is a three-part, sectional-like structure approximately as wide as the bunk beds are long. The left third of the structure has two lockers stacked with an open rectangular cube on top for towels, underwear, and other items and a smaller open rectangular cube on the bottom just above the floor. The middle section is a desk and folding chair. It also has a shelf above the desk area. The right section has another open cube on top and an open closet for hanging pants, shirts, dry coats. Shoes and the like for the lower bunk person are stacked under the hung clothes. Under the lower bunk can be placed musical instruments (one per inmate), shoes and footwear for the upper bunk, and laundry bags.

In some prison camps, your living area will be shared with three other bunk beds, making the living space 8´ X 16´ (see drawings on pages 48 and 49).

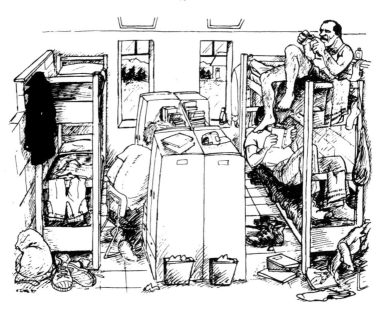

WHERE YOU KEEP YOUR PERSONAL PROPERTY

Toilet articles and issued medications go in your lockers. Commissary items are limited to no more than the monthly spending limit. You can have only two packs of cigarettes on your person, and no more than four cartons in your locker. You are allowed tennis and racquetball racquets, tennis balls, and handballs, and they must be stored in the clothes-rack section of the cubicle.

HOW MUCH MONEY CAN YOU HAVE?

At some, but not all camps, you are allowed to have up to $15 in postage stamps, $20 in nickels, dimes and quarters. You can have no more than $20 with you at any time. Possession of folding money will result in being shipped out to a higher-level prison.

A few camps do not allow convicts to have any money whatsoever.

CAN YOU HANG UP PHOTOS?

You cannot hang or tape calendars, or photographs, or any other items on lockers or your cubicle walls. You can display two picture frames, but they must be of the type sold in the commissary.

WHAT ABOUT YOUR WATCH?

With a Form #40 and/or a commissary receipt as proof of ownership, you may possess a radio and a watch. The radio cannot have a tape recording device, and you must have earphone adapters. The radio cannot be worth more than $75, and the watch cannot be worth more than $50.

HOW MUCH MAIL CAN YOU KEEP?

You can keep no more than a shoeboxful of mail with you. This is about 25 letters. When this limit has been reached, you should mail the lot of it to someone who will keep it for you.

WHAT IS CONTRABAND?

Contraband is anything that you did not purchase at the commissary, have issued to you by the government, or have an authorization for. Contraband includes articles of clothing in excess of allowed limits. It includes articles used for unauthorized purposes.

CUBICLES WILL BE SEARCHED FOR CONTRABAND

From time to time, the guards will search all cubicles for contraband. If you have so much as a flower petal, or a penny, you can be in serious trouble, depending on the sadism and/or stupidity of the guards. To be on the safe side, do not keep anything not expressly allowed in your cubicle.

DINING HALL RULES

The dining hall has many rules for conduct and dress, and these vary from camp to camp. You will not be allowed to smoke, whistle, or be boisterous in the dining hall. You will oftentimes not be allowed to wear shorts, shower or house shoes, hats, or sweat bands. You will sometimes be allowed to wear casual shirts, white t-shirts, jackets, and raincoats, and thermal underwear.

HOW IS THE FOOD?

The menu is not terrible, but it does resemble hospital food. It is served cafeteria style.

WHAT IF YOUR RELIGION HAS FOOD RULES?

Pork items are marked with an * for those with religious restrictions. You can observe your religious dietary laws if you send a signed request to the chaplain.

CAN YOU TAKE FOOD OUT OF THE DINING HALL?

The only food item that can be taken out of the dining hall is fresh fruit. Generally speaking, you can take one piece of it out onto the base, but you may return none of it to camp. Enforcement of such rules varies.

MEDICAL DEPARTMENT

The medical department of the camp will serve you for sick-call, emergencies, first aid, and routine treatment and follow-up care which is prescribed by the physician assistants or the chief medical officer. Sick-call hours are on the daily schedule. If you have an emergency or a scheduled appointment, it will be handled at other times than sick-call.

SICK-CALL APPOINTMENTS

If you need dental treatment, an eye examination, or glasses, such concerns will be handled through a sick call appointment. If you need eyeglasses, they will be prescribed and ordered at no cost to you. It will take two or three weeks for them to be ready for you. Contact lenses are not provided, neither is contact lens cleaning solution. The wearing of contact lenses is not encouraged, partially because of eye safety concerns in the event tear gas is deployed against convicts.

ELECTROCARDIOGRAMS

If you have reached age 50, you can have an electrocardiogram, and you will be offered tonometry and sigmoidoscopy. These procedures will be done only with your consent. The sigmoidoscope cannot be used only to search for contraband. If you are age 50 and have been in the institution for a year, you will be offered an annual physical examination. The medical care is generally low-rate, not high-tech.

PHYSICAL EXAMINATIONS

If you are being released from prison and your discharge date is not within a year of your previous physical examination, you may have a new physical examination upon request to the hospital staff. These exams will be conducted within two months prior to your release and will include the procedures performed on an admission physical examination. Other physical examinations are available for inmates if medically indicated, and your evaluations or declines of evaluations will be noted in your medical records.

DENTAL CARE

Dental sick call is provided if you are experiencing emergencies. Dental emergencies include toothaches, broken dentures that lacerate the mouth, swelling in the jaw or gums that is painful or distorting the face, complications from previous treatment, and other things that the examiner thinks require immediate attention.

Not included as dental emergencies are: lost fillings without pain, bleeding gums, tooth cleanings, pain when eating or drinking hot or cold foods, lost tooth or denture(s), uncemented crowns, and other problems that don't require immediate attention.

If you require non-emergency dental treatment, your name will be chosen in turn from treatment lists. You must submit an "Inmate Request to Staff Member" so that you will be added to the treatment list. If you need to have your teeth cleaned, for example, you must request that the dentist clean your teeth. About three months later, you might get your appointment. Normally, you will not get an appointment to get your teeth cleaned until you are preparing for your release from prison.

TRY NOT TO GET YOUR TEETH PULLED

Most prison dentists prefer to pull teeth rather than repair them. These dentists often promise dentures to their patients, dentures which never materialize. Many inmates have all of their teeth pulled by prison dentists, and never do get the dentures that they were promised.

DENTAL SICK CALL

Dental sick-call is often held on Monday through Friday at 1500 hours. Those on work details outside of the camp often have to sign up at the camp hospital between 0600 and 0615. If you work within the camp, you are often given an appointment time if you telephone the camp hospital between 0715 and 0815. These sick-call and appointment times vary from camp to camp, of course.

IDLE OR CONVALESCENCE STATUS

Idle: You must remain in your quarters except to go to meals, medication line, religious services, approved visits, medical call-outs, clothing exchange, sick-call and commissary. You will be prohibited from participating in any recreational activities outside your quarters. If your idle slip is marked "bed rest," you are restricted to your bed for medical reasons. You will be given a slip that says "Idle," and you must post this above your bed. Now you enter a game with the guards. The hacks love to catch "idle" convicts outside of their beds. If they catch an "idle" convict outside of bed, they write him up for violating the rules. This is called "getting a shot." Most times, the convicts on "idle" are faking it to avoid work, but they still like to work out in the weight room.

Convalescence: You do not participate in any work assignment, but you are not restricted to your quarters. You may not participate in strenuous activity. You may participate in chess, checkers, and cards. If you are enrolled in a school program, you may attend class only if your form indicates that you may attend class. Convalescent status is a desirable classification because it means that you won't have to work for up to six months.

Medical restrictions: You will be on work or athletic restriction after your initial physical examination if necessary, or upon discovery of disease or injury.

PSYCHOLOGY SERVICES

The camp has a licensed clinical psychologist on staff, as well as consulting mental health counselors. They are available for evaluation, crisis intervention and psychotherapy.

The department also coordinates a drug-abuse program. First priority for participating in this program is given to convicts with court recommendations for drug treatment in prison and convicts with histories of severe drug abuse problems. Such programs as drug education, Alcoholics Anonymous, Narcotics Anonymous and even personal development groups are offered for you.

During A & O, you will be screened by Psychology Services. But to make an emergency appointment, request that any staff call Psychology Services. To request non-emergency appointments, you should submit an "Inmate Request to Staff Member" to Psychology Services. A callout appointment will be made for you.

PSYCHOLOGICAL ASSISTANCE MAY BE ACCEPTABLE OR NONACCEPTABLE

At some prison camps, convicts do not use the services of the psychology department. If an inmate uses these services, he is labeled "crazy."

However, at other prison camps, the psychology department is THE place to be. If you do NOT use these services, the other convicts label you "crazy." Basically, this means that every institution is different. Figure out what's acceptable behavior before you do anything concerning the psychology department.

ATTENDING RELIGIOUS SERVICES

Attendance at all religious functions is voluntary. But a full program of religious services is provided by the institution. No matter what your faith, you'll find a service. Also, at some camps, a full-time nondenominational chaplain is on duty to care for your spiritual needs.

CHOOSING YOUR PRISON RELIGION

At some camps, everybody claims to be Jewish. This is because on Friday night, some camps allow the Jewish convicts to leave the prison camp on a prison bus and attend religious services on the military base. Not only that, at these religious services, family members and friends can come to the chapel and take part with the convict. This is an extra visit, only supervised by the chaplain. The chaplain is not a guard, so he supervises very loosely. In addition to this, after the service, there are food and snacks. There are brownies, cakes, cookies, and even shrimp at times. (Shrimp, by the way, is not a Kosher food.) On special Jewish holidays such as Passover, very special food is provided and family members can attend. You need to consider such benefits as these when you are determining what your religious affiliation will be while you are in prison. At other camps, the Jewish convicts are not given services on the military base with food served afterward. Consequently, there are far less "Jews" at these camps.

THE CHAPLAIN CAN GRANT YOU SPECIAL BENEFITS

One convict said the first time he ever met the chaplain at his prison, the chaplain said that he lived in an apartment, but would like to move to a house. The chaplain said that he needed more money to do that. At that time, the convict was pretty ignorant. He did not understand that the chaplain was making him an offer and asking him for a "gift." Later on, the convict discovered that the chaplain often arranged for sexual visits between convicts and their girlfriends on the military base, for a price. You may want to speak with your chaplain privately and see if he makes you a similar offer. If he does, you would be well advised to politely decline it, pleading poverty, so as not to anger him. A chaplain of this sort is in a power position, and can harm you if he decides to do so, so there is no reason to incur his animosity. All such a person wants is money, and if he doesn't think you have any, will go on to the next victim.

TELEPHONE CALLS

Although telephone policies differ from camp to camp, in most instances the telephone pavilion or kiosk contains telephones for collect calls only. You cannot make credit card calls. You may not conduct business dealings on the phone. Three-way telephone calls are not allowed. You may not use toll-free numbers. You must notify the Control Room officer prior to placing a call and, unfortunately, all calls are subject to being monitored. At some prison camps, you will hear the telltale "beep" of recording equipment constantly during your calls. At other camps, you will never hear the "beep," although your calls will be monitored and recorded just the same.

You are not allowed to use camp telephones, except with the approval of the Unit Manager, and with a staff member present. You are never allowed to use a telephone on the military base. There is a telephone available outside the Control Center to call taxicabs or airlines in connection with furloughs, furlough transfers, or releases.

CHAPTER EIGHT
VISITING PRIVILEGES,
THE COMMISSARY

VISITORS

From 8:00 a.m. until 3:30 p.m. on Saturdays, Sundays, and federal holidays, you may have visitors. However, no one can visit you unless they are on your official visitor list, which is maintained by the prison. Your visiting list will be prepared during your first interview with your counselor, or maybe with your case manager.

PUTTING SOMEONE ON YOUR VISITOR LIST

When you put someone's name on your visitor list, the prison camp will mail a questionnaire to that person. The potential visitor must complete and return the questionnaire to the prison camp. Some of your relatives will be embarrassed to receive mail from a federal prison camp. So you probably should warn them ahead of time. If you want to add other friends and relatives to your visiting list, you have to use the "Inmate Request to Staff Member" form. You need to make these requests at least three weeks in advance of any planned visits by anyone not already on your visiting list. Special-visit requests should be made at least ten days in advance.

VISITS BY CHILDREN

Children under 16 or 18 (depending on the various camps' policies) must be accompanied by an adult who is approved to be on your visiting list. At some camps, only eight visitors, including children, are allowed to visit at one time.

VISITORS MUST BRING PHOTO ID

Your visitors must bring photo identification, such as a driver's license or a passport, and they must sign in before they are allowed to visit with you. The guards will check the photo identification with the official visitor lists before your visitor is allowed to see you.

DISPLAYS OF AFFECTION

After your visitors sign in, the guards will call you to report to the visiting room for your visit. All visits begin and end in the visiting room. At the very beginning and end of visiting hours, you may shake hands, kiss, and embrace within the bounds of good taste. But during visits, contact between you and your wife or girlfriend is limited to hand-holding and having your arm around the other's waist, upper back, or shoulder. Excessive displays of affection could result in termination of the visit, or in disciplinary action.

SEX DURING VISIT — TECHNICAL ASPECTS

It is customary at some prison camps to cut the pockets out of your pants so that you and your visitor can grope each other easily. At some camps, this is an accepted practice. However, at other camps, it is NOT allowable to cut your pants pockets out, and any cut pants will be confiscated. You will soon learn what is and is not acceptable.

Most sex during visits takes place sitting side-by-side on concrete benches at the outdoor visiting tables. Those convicts who engage in such escapades tell their wives or girlfriends to skip the underwear and wear those shorts/skirts combination garments that enable them to reach up their legs to their pussies without attracting much attention. If a woman wears a long top which is not tucked into her skirt, the convict can reach underneath her blouse and hold and squeeze her titties. Then she can reach into his cut-out pants pockets while he's groping her. She can rub his naked penis and jack him off. The convict should always have at least one handkerchief and a full can of soda with him for cleanups after a hand job. If the mess is pretty obvious on his pants, he just spills the soda on himself to disguise it. This charade fools no one, but is acceptable behavior at some camps. It is nothing more than a game which demeans everyone involved. It also gives the supervising guards the opportunity to apprehend a convict if they so choose, so one should keep that in mind before engaging in such activities. Is a quick hand job worth being shipped out? Maybe it's better to masturbate in privacy.

BRING QUARTERS FOR MACHINE FOOD DURING VISITS

Visiting rooms contain a long bank of ten or fifteen vending machines. This will be the only food available to any of you during the visit. Your visitors should remember to bring rolls of quarters to use in these machines.

BRING SOAP IF YOU LIKE TO BE CLEAN

It also helps to have your visitors bring those small bars of hotel soap, since the washrooms often have no soap at all. Sometimes it's necessary to bring enough toilet paper to meet any immediate needs.

SEATING ARRANGEMENTS IN THE VISITING ROOM

Tables and chairs are sometimes in the middle of the room. If this is the case, you will use these for playing cards or games and eating snacks and lunch. If your visitors arrive early, they can take their pick of the tables and chairs. Early visitors often try to save table and chair space for friends who arrive later.

More commonly, visitors and convicts are seated side-by-side on seats which do not allow for face-to-face visiting.

THE VISITING YARD

Outside the visiting room is a visiting yard. There will be concrete tables and concrete benches so that you and your guests can talk or play cards. Some visiting yards are boxed in, meaning they are surrounded by a tall wooden fence. Other visiting yards are large and open grassy areas surrounded by roads or sidewalks. Often, you will see other convicts walking past the visiting area.

YOU WILL BE SEARCHED BEFORE AND AFTER VISITS

You will be searched, and occasionally strip-searched, just before and immediately after your visits. At some camps, even if they strip-search you, they rarely make you take off your socks. At those camps, daring convicts can smuggle contraband in their socks. At other camps, they make you take your socks off, so sock-smuggling is impossible. Convicts who wish to use their female visitors to smuggle in drugs sometimes ask them to conceal the drugs inside of small balloons, which are held in the woman's mouth and transferred into the convict's mouth during a kiss. Then, after the visit is over and the convict has returned to his quarters, he causes himself to retch, and retrieves the drug-filled balloon. Sometimes he waits until it has passed through his bowels, and searches through his feces until he finds it. If the balloon bursts while inside the convict's alimentary canal, it will probably kill him if it's filled with cocaine, heroin, or methedrine. If it's filled with marijuana, it will just give him a good buzz. Again, the convict is taking a big risk by engaging in smuggling contraband, and it's not a recommended practice.

WHAT YOUR VISITOR CAN BRING INTO THE VISITING ROOM

Each prison sets its own rules for what a visitor can bring, and these rules are changed whenever the hacks feel like it. Visitors may be allowed to bring purses, tote bags, or possibly only see-through plastic zipper bags. What your visitors can bring will change from week to week without prior notice.

If your visitors bring a baby, they can usually bring items directly related to infant care into the visiting room. Sometimes the baby's stroller, diapers, bottles, baby food, changes of clothing, and blankets will be allowed into the visiting room. Chewing gum and cameras are not allowed. You and your visitors will be allowed to smoke in designated areas only. If your visitor leaves the visiting room, the visitor will not be allowed to come back that day.

At some camps, your visitors may go with you to religious services. In some instances, children may attend Sunday School while parents are attending church services.

WHAT YOU CAN BRING INTO THE VISITING ROOM

Procedures vary from camp to camp, but generally speaking, the only items that you can take into the visiting room are a comb, a handkerchief, matches, cigarettes, smoking materials, and religious medals. As you leave the visiting room, you must get rid of your cigarettes. You must carry your commissary card with you to your visit. The hacks will take it at the start of your visit, and they will keep it until your visit is over. Then they will return it to you.

OTHER FORMS OF SMUGGLING DURING VISITS

Sometimes a visitor can leave rolls of quarters or even contraband buried in the visiting yard during a visit. Then convicts can come to the visitors area after visiting hours and dig a bit to find the buried treasures. A visitor can bring forbidden items in baby strollers or diaper bags or baby bottles. During visits, a convict can toss contraband to convicts outside the visiting area. Items can be hidden in bushes for convicts to retrieve later. These are only a few of the possibilities, and all are a good way to get into trouble. You are playing the hacks' "game" when you allow yourself to get sucked into smuggling, and it's a big mistake. You're risking a lot, and with very little to be gained. If you get caught or snitched off, you will be sent to a facility that will make the prison camp seem like a day-care center, and you'll probably wind up doing more time than if you just chilled out and forgot about trying to put one over on the prison authorities.

VISITORS CAN BRING YOU NEW SHOES

Another good way to get in trouble is over shoes. When you need a new pair of shoes, one of your visitors can get some in your size. The visitor will need your guidance in order to mark your inmate number on the shoes in the correct place. Then your visitor simply wears the new shoes into the visiting room. At the visit, everyone takes off their shoes. Then, when your visitor leaves, you simply trade: the guest puts on your old shoes and you wear the new ones. Contraband can be hidden in the new shoes. During searches, you have to remove your shoes, but convicts report that they have never seen the hacks rip a shoe apart looking for contraband.

Anyone dumb enough to engage in fruitless activities such as shoe-swapping probably deserves to be kept on ice in prison. No survivor would attempt such a boneheaded stunt if he truly cared about his freedom or the lives of his loved ones who are awaiting his return to the outside world.

COMMISSARY

You will be given a commissary account. The money you brought with you goes into this account. Deposits to your account may be made by cash, U.S. postal money orders, bank or store money orders, and personal checks. Except for cash and U.S. postal money orders, all other deposits are subject to a thirty-day hold prior to being posted to your account register number. To avoid this thirty-day hold, be sure that anyone who sends you money sends it in the form of a U.S. postal money order. Your complete name must be on the check or money order. All money orders and checks must be sent through the mail.

The Commissary acts as a banking facility for all inmates' funds. Deposits are from performance pay and money which comes in the mail. Withdrawals are from commissary sales slips or Form 24s, which are used for furlough money, organizational memberships, etc.

YOU WILL ONLY BE ABLE TO SHOP ONCE A WEEK

The Commissary is open Monday through Friday on a schedule. You may make purchases only once a week. Your accounts will be checked at open house or else by using automatic electronic machines, which almost never seem to work.

Practices vary, but oftentimes you will be allowed a maximum of $105 per month in purchases, plus a maximum of $80 on special orders. You can order hobby items, sports shoes, tennis racquets, and other articles costing more than $25.

HOW YOUR COMMISSARY ORDER IS FILLED

You are given a pre-printed commissary list in advance of shopping. You take your pen and make check marks on a pre-printed commissary list, indicating how much of each item you wish to buy. Then you go to the commissary window and give your list to a convict. The convict places the things you ordered into little grocery baskets. The baskets are loaded onto a long conveyor belt. The officer in charge of the commissary rings you out, sort of like at a grocery store. The officer checks your commissary account to be sure that you have enough money in it to pay for your purchases. He also checks that you haven't gone over your monthly maximum in purchases. Among the things you can buy are these:

sodas

fruit juices

tea bags and coffees

hot cocoa

sugar cubes and
   sugar substitutes

nondairy creamers

vitamins

protein powder

athletic supporters

tennis balls

racquet balls

shower shoes

instant soups

ramen noodle soups

instant oatmeals

cookies, crackers, cakes
   such as Chips Ahoy, sal-
   tine crackers (salted and
   unsalted), Ritz crackers,
   pecan cookies, iced oat-
   meal cookies, goldfish
   crackers, chocolate or
   vanilla snack cakes,
   Swiss Cake rolls

snacks

picante sauce

peanut butter

onion dip

cheese bar with jalapenos

beef summer sausages

white tuna

jalapeno peppers

steak

sardines in oil

fish

aftershave lotion

deodorant

baby powder, foot powder

Noxzema

petroleum jelly

baby oil

sunblock

hair dressings

plastic spoons

combination lock (you need
   one of these)

toenail clippers

cups

cigarette case

photo album

writing pads

book light

picnic jug

Kleenex

large and small picture frames

shampoos	sun glasses
toothpaste	soaps
fruit	laundry soap
matches	chewing tobacco, pipe tobacco,
ice cream or ice cream bars	cigarettes
chips and pretzels	yogurt
tennis socks	tube socks
Bic pen	locker mirror
playing cards	chapstick
cotton-tipped sticks	sewing kits
razors	headbands
shoelaces	stereo headphones
shoe polish	booklight bulbs
mustache scissors	tennis string
sunflower seeds	raisins
candies	cashew pieces
toothbrushes	batteries
cough drops	weightlifting gloves

BUYING MONEY AT THE COMMISSARY

At some prison camps, you can purchase coins from the commissary for use in vending machines. You may buy $15 worth of rolled coins in nickels, dimes, and quarters denominations. Other prison camps do not allow convicts to possess any money at all.

At some prison camps, you may carry only $20 worth of coins on your person and you may have a total of only $20 in your possession at any time. If you are working on a base detail, you may have only $1 in your possession while on the base working. If you are working in camp details which permit you to go on base, you may not have more than $1 in your possession while on base.

OTHER COMMISSARY SERVICES

You may contribute to political parties or candidates. You may order flowers sent by telegraph delivery. You may participate in the U.S. Savings Bond Program.

YOUR RADIO

You may purchase a radio from the commissary. The radio must be inscribed with your register number at the time of its purchase. You cannot accept a radio as a gift from another convict. You cannot carry your radio to your job assignment. You must use earphones when playing your radio in buildings or any other areas which could disturb others. You may play your radio outside the dormitories but only at a volume that does not disturb others.

Earphones can be extremely loud. Some convicts crank up their radios as high as possible through the earphones, and this can be disruptive to those around them. Try not to play your radio so loudly that you disturb others.

OTHER MUSICAL INSTRUMENTS

You may play nonelectric guitars and harmonicas in the music room or outside the dormitories as long as you are not disturbing others. You must store your guitar under the bed in an enclosed guitar case. Even acoustic music can be annoying to others, so try not to bother others with your musical endeavors.

OUTGOING MAIL

You are allowed to send outgoing mail. It should be sealed, and the hacks have the right to open it if they are in the mood. Most of the time, your outgoing mail is not unsealed and read. However, if you are being targeted for an investigation, your outgoing mail certainly will be unsealed and examined carefully by the guards.

INCOMING MAIL

Your incoming mail will always be opened before you get it. The authorities at your federal prison camp will search it for contraband and unauthorized material. Here are some examples of unauthorized material: body hair, small artifacts, plant shavings, sexually explicit personal photographs, cassette tapes, musical cards, stamps, stationery, envelopes, lottery tickets, plastic cards. The hacks will enjoy any sexually explicit photos that are sent to you, but you will never see them yourself. All unauthorized material is sent back to the sender with an official form from the U.S. Department of Justice stating what was returned and why.

MAIL IDENTIFICATION

All mail that you send or receive must contain the following information:

Name
Register Number
P.O. Box Whatever
FPC Wherever
Zip Code

YOU CAN'T RECEIVE STAMPS

You will not be allowed to receive stamps or stamped items such as envelopes embossed with stamps or postal cards with postage already affixed.

RECEIVING NEWSPAPERS

You may receive newspapers only if they come to you directly from the publisher.

RECEIVING BOOKS

You may receive hard-cover books directly from the publisher, a bookclub, or a bookstore. You may receive softcover materials such as paperback books and magazines from any source, but the packing material must not resemble a package. Usually there is a limit of five books per envelope.

RECEIVING MAGAZINES

You may subscribe to magazines. Your correctional counselor can give you a Form 24 so that you can get your subscription to magazines.

RECEIVING PACKAGES

Some prison camps do not allow convicts to receive packages. Others do. At such camps, packages require pre-authorization. One convict reports that his sister sent him a box of paperback books, but they were sent back to her as unauthorized because they were packed in a box. His sister repacked them into big envelopes, and he got them.

If you need to receive a package, you must get an authorization from your Unit Team, Education, Chaplain, or the Medical Department. The signed authorization will be placed on file and a copy of it must be enclosed with the package.

Then when the package arrives in the Mail Room, the guards will compare the authorization to the package received.

RECEIVING LEGAL MAIL

Legal Mail and Special Mail are treated differently. The sender must be adequately identified and the firm identified on the envelope. The envelope itself must be marked "Special Mail - Open Only in the Presence of the Inmate." Otherwise, it will be treated as general correspondence.

CUSTODY

You are assigned to "Out Custody" when you arrive at the federal prison camp. This means that you are correctly placed at a Level 1 institution. To get into any community-based activity, including furloughs and halfway house, you must obtain community custody. Your team can grant you this after you have been at the FPC for a specific length of time.

CHAPTER NINE
LONELINESS, CONFUSION, AND DESPAIR

DIP RECIPE

In the evening, and for going-away parties (when someone is being released from prison), convicts prepare the infamous "inmate dip." All of the ingredients can be purchased at the Commissary, if you do not have a friend in Food Service. Here is the recipe:

1 pack of Ramen noodles
1 pop-top can of white tuna
1 jar of Cheez Whiz
Jalapeno peppers if obtainable
Saltines or Ritz crackers

Get a bowl from your locker. Cook the Ramen noodles using the hot water tap at the water fountain. Drain out the water and dump the noodles into your bowl. Mix in the can of white tuna, the jar of Cheez Whiz, and Jalapeno peppers.

Dip crackers into the bowl of concoction and enjoy. This recipe makes enough to share with 3 or 4 inmates.

When you get out of prison, you will probably make this dip for your family one evening. It won't taste as good as it did in prison camp.

GET INFORMATION ABOUT YOUR PRISON CAMP

When you are first assigned to a prison camp, you need to find out as much about it as possible. Your best bet for information is to try to talk to convicts who have just gotten out of that particular prison camp. However, if this is not possible, you should ask the other convicts who the "mayor" is. A "mayor" is a convict who considers himself a helper type. He wants to help other convicts with information. In return, the mayors are looking for people with money who can help them when they get out. Generally, they think they can tell you all about the camp.

LOSS OF PERSONAL SPACE

In prison, you are never alone. Everywhere you go, there are three or four or more people around you. For men who are accustomed to more personal space, this is a hard adjustment. If you are a man who enjoys his own personal time, it will be difficult to share every moment with others. You will have virtually no "me-time" to laugh or cry in private. It is a personal space nightmare.

In addition, it is in your best interest to be courteous to your fellow convicts, according to the unwritten code that you all are forced to live by. Don't demean other convicts, or make fun of them, even if they are clearly foolish. Don't throw your weight around, or flaunt your education or financial resources. You are all members of the convicted class, and in that respect you are all equals. Don't ever forget that.

WHAT ARE YOU IN FOR?

Everybody is going to ask you what you are "in" for. They want to know what crime brought you to prison camp. But they don't want a long explanation. They want a short summary. You need to have a one- or two-sentence explanation of your crime and your time. For example, "I was caught with 100 pounds of marijuana, and I've got a five-year top." Or, "I got three years for Medicare fraud." Don't elaborate unless asked, and even then don't offer any more information than is civil and polite. People can easily come to believe that you snitched people off in order to get into prison camp if you are not careful. Always act as if you expect to do your entire stretch, and you'll be better off. Be careful what you say, and think it out!

CHAPTER TEN
MAINTAINING YOUR RELATIONSHIPS

Over 85% of all marriages fail when one partner goes to prison. Fifty percent of those that do not fail during the incarceration period go on to fail within one year of the inmate's release. If you want to try to beat those odds, there are several things that you can do.

WRITE A LOT OF LETTERS

Write to your wife and children regularly and often. This will help you to express your feelings and to deal with the boredom. Your wife will love receiving the letters, and so will your children. When your wife gets mad at you, she can refuse to open your letters for a day or two. Ask her to save all of them as valuable family history.

MAKE PHONE CALLS

It will be helpful for you, in addition to the daily letters, to maintain voice communication. Call your family every night.

Of course, the only way you can call is collect. This adds up to tremendous phone bills, which is one more reason why you may need to get rid of your assets and convert them to cash.

You can manage to call home twice a day if you give it some planning. You can only really call home between 6 and 9 p.m. because during the other phone hours, you are supposed to be working. The phone area is not the most pleasant place. At a typical camp there is one phone available for every sixty inmates. The phones are outdoors. You stand in line for your turn at the phone. You are allowed a fifteen-minute phone call on the honor system, which never works. The normal wait is anywhere from thirty minutes to an hour. Therefore, between 6 and 9 at night, you could get two phone calls made if you started lining up at 5:30.

Having the phones out in the open is no fun when it rains. Standing in line in the rain, you will get soaked to the skin. And the phone lines and phone calls are a source of constant heated arguments. Phone-call regulations vary from camp to camp. In many cases, convicts theoretically sign in when they are first in line, and put down the times when they start their phone calls. In practically, they write down the times as being 15 or 20 minutes later than the times they actually start their calls. Occasionally, a hack will come by, look at the list, and kick everybody off the phones for lying. There will be a guard stationed in a phone room at all times, eavesdropping and recording all conversations.

It is easy to forget that your calls are being monitored. So if you are talking dirty with your wife, expect the hacks to hear it. In some instances, the hacks will make lewd comments to you the next time they see you, just to let you know that they are privy to your conversations.

HAVE WEEKLY VISITS

If you are hoping to maintain a good relationship with your wife and children, communication is essential. Letters help; phone calls help; but if you want your children to see you and to know you, weekly visits are extremely important. When your prison camp is on a military base, there will be regularly scheduled airplane flights and bus stops nearby. There will be motels that cater to weekend prison-camp visitors by accepting collect calls. You can ask other inmates for the names of these motels if you didn't scout out the area before you arrived.

YOU MAY WANT TO MOVE YOUR FAMILY CLOSER

It is much easier for your family to visit if they live nearby. Quantity time and quality time are your goals here. When you get out, your family will feel much closer to you if they've seen you every weekend. Some families visit all day on both days each weekend. Some families visit all day for one day. Some just drop in for an hour or so. But the families that visit have a better chance of staying together.

There is another benefit to moving your family closer. Having your family live locally allows you to use the special "local" phones. In general, prisons provide phones reserved for local residents. "Locals" have their own separate phone line, and as long as no one is behind you, you can stay on for as long as you want. And the cost of the phone call is a flat charge instead of a time-related charge.

Of course, it is not always feasible or practical for your family to move closer to your prison camp. There are a lot of variables to take into consideration. But if it is possible, and will not disrupt your wife's work or your children's schooling, you may want to pursue this option.

HOW TO MAKE VISITS FAMILY TIME

At some prison camps, your wife can pack books, crayons, playing cards, and little activity books for the children to bring into the visiting room. One convict reports that at first the hacks allowed children and their daddies to play tossing games with fuzzy tennis balls and Velcro mitts. Then when the hacks saw that the families were having fun and not bothering anyone, they stopped the games. The fuzzy tennis balls were banned.

At some camps, your wife could try to bring colored chalk so you and your kids can draw pictures on the sidewalk of the visiting area. The hacks might stop you. But they might not.

Sometimes, to amuse yourself and your children, you read them books, play cards with them, and help them color pictures. They will learn how to operate a wide variety of vending machines and how to watch out that someone doesn't cheat them out of their quarters. You will be able to maintain a decent relationship for your entire sentence. Of course, many prison camps have very strict visiting procedures, and none of the activities mentioned above are possible. You'll have to wait and see what the rules are in the camp at which you'll be doing time.

ASK YOUR FAMILY TO BE SUPPORTIVE
OF YOUR WIFE

It is good if your wife's family can be supportive and helpful financially. But if your in-laws are typical, they may not have approved of you to start with. You might not have been "good enough" for their perfect little girl. Of course, they were nice to you when you were providing money. But now that you're in the slammer, they might not be so friendly.

If your wife's family won't be supportive, at least your family should be. After all, she is taking care of their grand-children and their son. They should call her every so often. They should try to send money and presents to your children, and they should try to visit you. If they act unsupportive, it will be so much easier for your wife to listen to her side of the family. And her side will NOT be encouraging her to stick by you. That's why it is so important for your side to help her. It is really in their best interests to encourage your wife not to divorce you right now. And, believe me, there will be plenty of times when she will want to divorce you.

PRISON IS STRESSFUL FOR YOUR FAMILY, TOO

Losing a husband to the federal prison system is different than losing a spouse through death or divorce. With death, there might be life insurance to collect and use to survive fi-nancially. And the family doesn't have to consider moving closer to the cemetery so that the children can visit Daddy all day every Saturday and Sunday.

Remember that your wife needs to have your thanks and your recognition for her contribution toward keeping your family together. As one convict said, you should act like you are interested in her problems, even if you aren't.

OTHER INMATES' WIVES MAY BE CON ARTISTS

There may be a group of convicts with local families who are willing to help your wife. This can be very helpful, and it is definitely something to look into. Of course, sometimes these "prison-support groups" are just scams, perpetrated by predatory individuals, so don't rely on them without first determining their validity. Tell your wife to be careful.

CHAPTER ELEVEN
DOING YOUR OWN TIME

There is an old saying that convicts have been repeating for many years: "Do your own time. Don't do anyone else's." Ultimately, what you do with your time is up to you. You can network, because many of the inmates will not be leaving the life of crime. They will have plans for you to listen to. Just be careful that you are not the one being scammed, because they will be eager to find new people to run scams on. A lot of inmates will ask you to send money to them when you get out. You can make plans to get together after you've served your time. Remarkably, once you are released, you will find that in most instances you will have very little interest in rekindling your prison-camp friendships. And, until you are released from probation/parole, you are not supposed to associate with other convicted felons.

There are other alternatives, too. You can stay by yourself and read books. The prison library has many paperback and hard-cover books. You can catch up on all the reading you missed out on, and hopefully improve your mind. At the very least, you can read as a diversion.

At many camps, you can work out with weights and improve your physical body. You can walk or run on the track. You can play tennis. Sometimes there are yoga and aerobics classes available. Your health improvements will be worth the effort.

Or you can use the time to better your mental skills. Many prison camps have college-credit courses that you can take to improve your educational skills. They often have vocational classes that you can take to improve your motor and mental skills. It is up to you.

You will have so much time on your hands. It's a shame to waste it.

SNITCHES AND SET-UPS

In a low-level prison, you need to realize that snitches are everywhere. In a high-level prison, snitches may be murdered. At a camp, that fear is not as great, and is, in fact, rather unlikely. Since snitching is so prevalent, and the snitches don't have to worry very much about repercussions, there are oftentimes set-ups that are designed to trap you. And these set-ups will become more frequent as you get "shorter" (closer to release.) The other convicts, and especially the hacks, get a perverted thrill from watching you suffer.

EVERYTHING COULD BE A SET-UP

Former PTL official Richard Dortch, in his book *Integrity*, says that when he was serving his time in Eglin Federal Prison Camp, the chaplain tried to shake him down for computers for the chaplain's home and for tuition for the chaplain's child's schooling. Dortch was very paranoid, was becoming a short-timer, and was deeply afraid that it was a set-up.

Be especially careful as you get really short. At that time, everything probably *is* a set-up. This is the time when you are in the most danger. Be sure to keep your locker locked, so that it will be harder for others to steal your belongings or plant contraband.

When a convict is short, the predators are more likely to take their shot at him. They know that a short-timer is so desperate to get out that he is less likely to fight back and be disciplined. Rapes are not common in prison camps, but this is when the majority of them occur. The disgruntled convicts who have been nursing grudges deliver their paybacks at this time, too. Watch yourself, and try not to give anyone the opportunity to take advantage of you.

A FAVORITE SET-UP

Every prison camp has its favorite set-ups. Here is how one set-up worked. We'll call the set-up artist Bobby the Snitch. Bobby liked to inform a newer prisoner with on-base duty that Bobby and the other prisoners could arrange a conjugal visit for the new man and his girlfriend. During visiting hours, the new prisoner and his girlfriend were instructed about the plan and how it worked. The girlfriend was told to come to the area on Thursday of the coming week and to check into a specific motel and wait. The prisoner, who worked outside the prison camp on the military base, would be picked up at his work site and transported to the motel for a few hours of wild sex. Unfortunately, when the prisoner was dropped off, he was met by not only his girlfriend, but also by waiting prison hacks, who had been alerted to his plans by Bobby and the other snitches. And the next thing the convict knew, he was shipped.

A SET-UP THAT DIDN'T WORK

Bobby the Snitch's plans didn't always work. One new convict was assigned a job at the edge of the woods on the military base. It was about a mile away from the prison camp itself. Bobby the Snitch told the inmate that he should have his wife meet him in the woods for sex the next Tuesday morning. The convict's wife drove to a deserted picnic area in the woods. There she changed into jogging clothes, and ran into the woods. The convict was waiting for her among the trees, and they dropped their pants and fucked on the forest floor. The convict reports that it's a good thing that the sex didn't last more than a minute, because almost before they were done, the woods became deathly still. There was no noise at all, not even a bird chirping, and they were terrified. The convict jumped to his feet, zipped up his pants, and raced back to his job site. On the way, he said that he could hear voices on walkie-talkies from somewhere nearby in the forest. Meanwhile, his wife pulled up her shorts and hurried as fast as she could in the other direction. It turned out to be a damn good thing that the convict did not walk his wife back to her car like a gentleman.

As the wife reached the edge of the woods, she saw a white pickup truck parked across the small parking lot opposite from her car. It was backed into a parking spot, and she said that she made sure that she didn't even look at the pickup as she jogged innocently out of the woods and then stopped on the asphalt to time her heartbeat with her wristwatch...just as if she were the most clueless jogger in the world. Then she ambled over to her car and changed her clothes, hoping that the occupant of the white truck wasn't some deranged character from *Deliverance*, or, worse, a hack.

It turned out to be a hack. He followed her car all the way to the edge of the military base as she left, and then he returned to confront the convict, who by now was back at his post. "I don't know what the fuck you were doing back there," he barked to the convict. "But it had better never happen again. If I ever catch your wife on base again when it's not visiting hours, I'll ship you that very day."

The convict said that he never trusted Bobby the Snitch again.

CHAPTER TWELVE
DAY BY DAY IN FEDERAL
PRISON CAMP

EXCERPTS FROM PRISONERS' JOURNALS

These are excerpts from journals written by convicts who recently served time in the federal prison-camp system. Of course, the names have been changed. As you will see, you can learn from the other convicts. Each of them has a story, and each of them has advice that they may be willing to share with you. Although experience is the best teacher, you can learn from someone else's experience, too.

10-24: My roommate told me I was snoring last night. He said that sometimes people will throw things at inmates who snore — things like tennis balls or toilet paper rolls.

I tried playing some bridge. They take it very seriously here. I bid wrong and everybody told me how I was doing it wrong. They told me what bridge guidebooks I should read. Then they informed me that the beginners' bridge class was coming up on Saturday morning and I should definitely be there.

My roommate had me practice getting in and out of bed so that I won't disturb him as he lies in the bottom bunk.

Tomorrow is inspection day, so we have to clean our floor and make sure that the towels are folded correctly. The bed must be made tight enough that a quarter will bounce on it. It is so cold at night that I sleep in my sweatsuit and socks.

10-26: I will never forget the end of my first visiting day. My wife brought our two toddlers. When the visit was over, and it was time for me to go, they screamed for me, "Daddy! Daddy! Daddy, don't go! Daddy, don't go! Don't leave!" It broke my heart.

I had dinner with a guy who is in prison for price-fixing fish in Maine. He pleaded guilty and received six months.

I walked over to the woodworking shop to see it. The inmates were making a lot of bowls and other wooden things. I asked one of them if there was a class offered in woodworking, and he snapped, "NO!" Inmate Frank told me that they sold the bowls "off the books" and didn't want any more competition.

I hear that this prison camp is where the Bureau of Prisons sends the people who are under protective custody under assumed names.

10-28: All of the different departments like laundry or shoes are run by inmates. There is a civilian worker there, too, but usually that civilian person chooses to do nothing. So what happens is that the inmate in charge of that department hands out whatever he can to his friends for free. Then he charges all the rest of the inmates.

At lunch I sat with some guy, and I asked about Inmate Bobby, a guy who Ira said was a snitch. This guy said no, Inmate Bobby is not a snitch but Ira is a snitch. Everybody calls someone else a snitch from time to time. Ron, another Jewish inmate, who is about seventy years old, lectured me and said that I should never say anything bad about another inmate. Then Edgar told me that Ron was correct, but Ron is a snitch.

10-29: Today starts A & O lectures and tests. If you do not pass the tests you have to go to night school.

The Silver Bullet bus came in last night with ten to fifteen new inmates.

Delmar, the inmate with the house, asked me if I had started my diet yet. Just because I gained sixty pounds in four months after losing my trial... I am not sure that I am ready to diet yet.

I had my first A&O lecture today. The administration just stood there feeding us a lot of crap about how they are here to help us and if we need anything at all we should let them know. Sure.

Spitting is a big hobby here. Most inmates walk around spitting all over the place, sort of like a dog pees to mark its territory.

I will try to get a haircut later, but evidently there are not any actual hours when the barbers are there. The barbers come to work when they feel like it. Also, I heard that you have to pay the barber with money to get a haircut, even though it is supposed to be free.

10-30: I got back from my physical, and I received a slip for a lower bunk, and I have a twenty-pound weight restriction. I received the lower bunk slip because, when I first checked in, I answered a series of questions, and one of the questions was, "Do you sleep walk?" Well, I answered "yes," and now that means that I am a hazard to be on a top bunk. I now have to wait until a bunk becomes available. The twenty-pound weight restriction came about because of the letter our family doctor wrote to say that I had a knee problem and should not lift objects over twenty pounds.

The laundry washes your institutional clothing for you. Nevertheless, several inmates hire another inmate to wash their clothing and make their beds. It is off-the-books and it usually costs about sixty dollars a month for that service. The paying inmate has someone on the outside mail the payment money to the other inmate by sending it either to his family or to his commissary account. Some inmates make a thousand dollars a month this way.

I went to make a phone call, but the phones were not turned on, even though they are supposed to be turned on at 8 a.m. Someone told me that every time a Silver Bullet bus pulls out, the phones are turned off so that the inmates cannot call someone on the outside to ambush the Silver Bullet. After five to eight hours, the phones are turned back on.

10-31: I finally got my hair cut. The barber was a pilot who ran drugs. He got fifteen years with no parole. He said he was in a higher-level prison in another location first and he liked it there. He said that there were inmates there who were serving three hundred years. They spent their whole life behind bars. He said that once a month on a weekend the hacks would give breath tests to the inmates for booze, and then the hacks would sell liquor to the inmates.

I heard that there is an inmate here who got one year for eating turtle eggs, and another who received eight months for taking trash from the post office. Mr. Postman worked at the post office, and he said that if there was no forwarding address on giveaways like CDs and such, the post office was supposed to throw them away. But instead, he went through the trash and took whatever he wanted. And that's why he is here.

The beds by the ice machine and the toilets are called waterfront property. They are considered the worst.

All federal holidays are visiting days here, so on Veterans Day you can visit.

Walking is a big thing here. Most inmates walk up and down the track just to do something, just like caged animals.

11-01: This place is a personal-space nightmare. Cliff, my bunkmate, is obsessed with keeping our little bunk super-clean. The first day I arrived, Cliff held up a bottle to my face, and asked me if I knew what was in the bottle. "Shampoo?" I guessed. "Yes," said Cliff, "but not the ordinary shampoo. It is shampoo that you cannot get." As if I cared about a special shampoo. I didn't know yet that anything that one inmate has and no one else has becomes very important.

Densch and Wilmer are trying to get congressmen to help them get out earlier. I told them that they should cool it or they would make the prison administration mad. They replied that they did not care and hoped that if they created enough stink that the judge would take pity on them and let them out. I remember when I thought like that.

11-02: Most of the inmates have similar stories about eating their "last supper" for months and gaining tons of weight. They say that their wives grumble that the inmate is killing himself, and that is what the government wants. Or the wife says, "Do you want your kids to see you like this?"

Yesterday the chaplain came over the loud speaker and said that someone had stolen the Moslem Holy Book, which is a huge book. Most of the inmates were laughing. The chaplain asked the inmate who stole it to return it.

11-04: I was talking to Inmate Stoner. He works in the food service. He says he is six feet, four inches, and when he came in, he weighed five hundred pounds. He said he usually weighs four hundred, but he gained one hundred pounds in eighteen months before he came in. Now he is back at his fighting weight of four hundred.

Ron, the seventy-year-old, says he used to be in the produce business. Then he got into the carpet business and ended up in here. He says he's here for tax evasion. His brother is in another penal institution. Ron's job is to clean the windows in the visitors' room. That is where all the officers hang out. So Inmate Ron is constantly talking to them. Inmate Ron always seems to know which officer has what duty before they report for duty. Most inmates do not talk freely with the hacks at all. It is frowned upon by the other inmates. Most inmates will not talk to inmates who talk to the hacks because they feel that if an inmate talks to a hack, that inmate is a snitch. Calling an inmate a snitch is the worst name you can call an inmate.

11-05: Today Densch gave me his tuna fish, since he hates it. You always try to find someone like Densch in the food line so you can get more food.

The guy who cut my hair told me that there are 11 guys in "The Hole," which is like jail here. If you get into discipline trouble, you are sent to The Hole. A guy who is a protected witness got into a fight. Mr. Protected Witness is a black belt in karate. He has been in fights and in The Hole before. And this time the guards put him in The Hole again. Well, Mr. Protected Witness ratted on everyone in the camp so he wouldn't get shipped to a higher-level prison. As a result, the military police raided all of the R&G crews that work on the military base. They broke into all of their sheds and found liquor, cocaine, illegal stoves, hot plates, and food. So they put a lot of R&G workers in The Hole. There was speculation about whether or not they would let Mr. Protected Witness out of The Hole again, or just ship him to another camp.

I played spades with Hilton the defrocked rabbi. He says he is an insurance man and had a broker's license. He had been in town for 15 years and was head of the insurance association's ethics committee for five years. Six years ago he was scammed by another broker who sold him bogus securities. This guy made up stationery from a real company and had a co-conspirator mail fake statements from where the real company was located. Hilton had twenty of his best clients invest $638,000 in the bogus mutual fund. One Friday, one of his clients called and asked him to redeem $10,000 of his investment. Hilton called the broker but could not get hold of him. So Hilton looked up the phone number to the real company and called it and asked for his contact there. The real company said that the broker did not work there. Then Hilton called the other number, and the secretary said, "Don't worry. The broker took care of it." Monday morning, when he came back to work, the broker's phone numbers were disconnected. Then Hilton took a gun, got on a plane, and went looking for the scam guy. He was on the road for three months looking for the scam guy, and finally gave up. He came home and decided to try to pay everyone back without going to the authorities. He took out a second mortgage on his house and said nothing to his wife. Then some other client called and wanted to redeem $45,000. So Hilton got some new clients to invest $45,000 to cover the redeemed money. After two years of this, he says he had paid back $508,000, but by then he had nine new investors. One of the nine new clients called the SEC and complained. Hilton took all of the information to the insurance commissioner whom he had known for 12 years. The insurance commissioner called the SEC and arranged a meeting. The FBI was at the meeting, and they taped it. They worked out a deal, and Hilton only got 15 months. His wife divorced him. His lawyer asked for $3,000, which was all Hilton had. Then two weeks later, the lawyer asked for another $10,000. Hilton fired him. Hilton said that in prison, the best you can ask for is to find one or two people you can trust and that you can talk to. Everyone else you stay away from. He says that the Jews are lucky at some prison camps, because the Rabbi does not work for the Bureau of Prisons, even though the Chaplain does.

I met a guy who said he had Diesel Therapy for eight months.

Aaron's mother had a bypass surgery, and I guess she was not doing well, so she is on a life-support machine. So far, the prison officials have not let him out to see her. I was talking with him and Emilio, the guy with the 16- month-old twins. Aaron said that he has to do all of his 24 months. Somehow, he lost all of his good time. It took him over one year to get community service, which normally takes six months. Emilio and Aaron were telling stories about how they went around stealing food on their R&G crew, and throwing the excess bottles and wrappers at parked autos.

Camp is abuzz about everybody being in The Hole, and the raiding of all the Roads and Grounds crews. I don't think they will let Aaron go see his mother because he has not been a good boy in camp. Emilio also is a bad boy, saying that he has been written up ten times for making mistakes. He says they brought him into camp because someone caught him with his wife when he had an on-base job. As a result of his dalliance, the hacks took him off the base job, and now he works in the prison camp.

I spent most of my time as an orderly for Hilton the Rabbi in Dorm 4. He says he still has to pay restitution of $106,000, and he owes the IRS $100,000. Everyone in here has serious money problems.

11-07: Here is the way they assign jobs in here. When an inmate has been taken off a job (because he is leaving or in the hospital or for whatever reason), then the other inmates on the crew start asking for their buddies to come and work with them. If Inmate X, the buddy, agrees, then the inmates on the crew tell the boss guard that Inmate X will make a good addition to the workforce. The boss guard calls Inmate X's unit team, and requests the new worker Inmate X. His unit team calls Inmate X in, and reassigns him. So the result is that the work forces are basically controlled by the inmates.

I also understand that certain jobs are kept for protected witnesses. These jobs are the easy ones — for example, one such job is to pass out lunch sandwiches to the crews going out onto the base between 7 and 7:30. If you have this job, you are off again until 12:30 when you clean up the room from which you load the trucks. That's all you do.

The manners in here are pretty frayed. Language is strong gutter. Everyone is a "cocksucker" and a "motherfucker." Wilmer, the inmate who checked in with me, says he cannot stand the burping and the farting.

Remember Mr. Postman, the postal worker who lived in a small town and had diesel therapy? He is also a minister, and now he is off of A & O and assigned to a job in the chapel. And now Mr. Postman thinks he is better than the other inmates. There is a custom here that the chaplain brings you a birthday card on your birthday. I mentioned to Mr. Postman that the chaplain had forgotten to bring my bunkie a birthday card on his birthday a few days ago. Mr. Postman turned to me and said, "Fuck you and fuck your bunkie." I mentioned it to Emilio, and he said that most of the white-collar type of criminals in prison think they are better than the rest of the inmates.

Tobacco smoke is thick in here. A lot of people smoke cigarettes and cigars, so the smoke is everywhere in this camp, even outdoors. I am glad I don't have asthma.

The whole camp is talking about an article in *Penthouse* magazine which says that Eglin Air Force Base is the best prison camp in which to serve your time. It has a picture of a man in a chair smoking a pipe, reading a book, with a glass of iced tea, and all of it is in front of a tennis court.

Remember all of the inmates who promised to help me get a job in the kitchen or the laundry or on their crew? I just got classified. I am on RG21. RG or Roads and Grounds, also known as "Real Good." This means that I clean up a parking lot at a shopping center. From what I understand, there are lots and lots of people and autos through the shopping center, and I, along with a couple of other inmates, try to keep it clean. I was offered the precious metals room, which I understand is a room with no heat or air conditioning. But you sit all day long, sorting gold and silver out of things like old computers. The metals room does not get to come into camp for lunch. You have to take a sandwich with you, instead. I said, "Give me a hot lunch," and they said, "RG21!" and that was the end of the meeting.

11-08: I had heard that inmates who get sick get shipped out to a higher-level prison. Hilton told me that the camp does ship some of the ill inmates, but they weren't just sick; they were sick and nonworking. Since this is technically a work camp, you have to work. When inmates say they are too sick to work at all, the prison ships some of them. Some people with illness get assigned to CCS2. That means that about all you can do is pick up butts inside the compound.

I think my job will be on the outside. That's not the best, but I will get to see real people. After a while, the people who stay on the inside get sort of strange and overly suspicious. I remember when I was working on the food line, and I said "thank you" to this guy Carl, since he was helping me. He finally told me to stop it. He said he has been down for three years, and that nobody has been kind to him, and he did not know how to respond when I said "thank you," and it made him uncomfortable. So I quit saying it.

By the way, Densch told me he got RG3. I hear RG3 is terrible. An RG crew is bad if the boss is bad. And this boss is supposed to be the worst. His crew has six openings out of ten. That is not a good sign.

Ricky who lives across the hall on the lower bunk is nervous. He had just come back from a ten-day furlough when the military police raids and the big arrests came down. Since then, the guards have not let him go out into the base to work. He thinks the inmates in The Hole are talking about him, implicating him in the crimes, snitching him out. He is 24 years old. He spent the last four years here, and he is about to get out in March. If he is implicated, he probably won't get out in March.

Delmar came in from work and told me that your phone is not working yet. He tried to call you from the forbidden phones outside the prison, on base, which is illegal. He got the word to me fast.

A new guy came in and said he got a three-year sentence for over five and a half kilos of cocaine. All the inmates think he is a snitch. If he asks a question, they just say, "Go ask the law library."

11-09: Wilmer had a visitor last weekend. At first, he said that his visitor was his girlfriend. Then he said that she is the ugliest of all his girlfriends. Then, after count, he said that she is not his girlfriend, she is his secretary. What's next? She's his mother??

A new older inmate, maybe 70 years old, was given a six-month sentence for something. He said he is not going to read a newspaper or watch the news on television, because "they" (the government) put him out of society. He was really going to teach "them" a lesson.

At dinner, they had some Chinese stuff they called pepper steak. I thought it was terrible, and could not eat it. Everyone else said it was great. I guess I have not been down long enough to appreciate prison cuisine.

Densch said that one of the guys in my dorm was involved with Ivan Boesky. He gets mail all the time and is in a single cubicle.

I was talking to Chris, the Michael Milken associate. He said he was waiting to go on home arrest. He said that the Bureau Of Prisons is expanding the home arrest from six months to eighteen months. He said that they were supposed to start this by the end of the year. He told me that I definitely should qualify for home arrest myself. It is an inmate rumor, and the inmate rumors are usually untrue. But it gave me hope.

I saw Aaron going to dinner. He just came back from his furlough to see his mother. I didn't think he would get the furlough.

Irvin, one of the new A & O's came in from a different institution. He has been down for about a year, and transferred. He said he was caught growing marijuana in his basement. He said the Feds got him by looking at his utility bills. At his trial, they based his sentence upon the fact that every plant was 2.25 pounds, which is really unrealistic. He is appealing that, so he spends a lot of time in the law library.

Elvis is a transfer from Rochester, and he is going to play bridge with me. He is sixtyish and received an eleven-year sentence. He said he was selling counterfeit birth control pills. He also says he is appealing his sentence. He is a very angry person. He complains about everything.

Randall, Wilmer's bunkmate, got four years for 500 grams of cocaine. He was supplying the nuclear plant where he worked.

Aaron told me that he was also on RG21. He gave me advice. (Everyone here gives me advice.) He says at first do not ask many questions, just be quiet. He said after a while they will tell you things once they get to know you. For example, they might tell me how I can buy pizza, how I can have sex visits, how I can get liquor.

11-15: Irvin, another guy in A&O, wanted to get classified into the kitchen. But he got RG21 instead. He was really pissed off. He said that the kitchen guard would get it all straightened out. He said that this guy had written a letter signed by the assistant warden to get Irvin on the kitchen crew. He was sure that by the weekend, he would be on the kitchen crew. Update: six months later, Irvin still had not been assigned to the kitchen crew.

Irvin came to my "house," or cubicle, to talk. He was talking about a higher-level prison, where he stayed for about a year. He said it was smaller, with a population of only 150 inmates. But the prisoners were rougher. He said that he was supposed to hand out only one piece of meat to inmates at meals. If somebody asked for two pieces, and he did not give the inmate two pieces of meat, he would get cussed out. And then the inmate would take a big shit in Irvin's bed. Irvin said this happened to him about twice a week.

I got transferred to a new cube on the bottom bunk. The cube was empty for about one week. So the other inmates have already stripped it clean. They even took the towel rack off the wall. They took the light bulb out of the desk lamp and switched out the desk with another crummier one. They even took out the starter mechanism for the fluorescent light.

I asked Irvin why his nurse-wife does not come up to visit him. And he gave me some feeble excuse that she was too broke. He says he really doesn't care because he believes that he is going to get out of prison in six months due to his appeal. A lot of inmates think that their appeals will be successful.

11-18: I saw some guys in the woods next to my job site. I asked one if he was looking for deer, and he answered, "Yes." I asked him if he needed help, and he said, "Not from you." His partner said that he would like help. He asked if I would chase the deer across the road, because it was against the rules to hunt deer where we were.

There is also a bulldozer out here. Today the military folks got it stuck again. They could not get it unstuck. This is a common occurrence, and it's always good for a laugh.

11-19: I talked to Delmar about the guys that I saw in the woods by my job site yesterday. He said they were some of the other prison bosses, and they were not supposed to be looking for deer, and I probably spooked them more than they spooked me.

Catty-corner from my "house" is a good laundry man. I told him that my blanket was stolen. And he told me (he speaks very little English) that he would get me two nice blankets for nothing. I guess that's how they try to get new laundry customers.

The other members of my work crew joke about the job that I have. Most of the other inmates declare that they could not stand all of that time spent alone. They consider it to be a lousy job because I don't get to see women.

I heard that the guards searched some lockers and found a $20 bill in one. Folding money is contraband. Folding money is not allowed.

Ray told me last night he was very happy that he has been cleared to go to work in the hospital on the air force base. Several other inmates told me that the hospital personnel treat the inmates very badly, but the inmates consider it a good job since it is indoors.

Here is Edgar's story. He says that he started out at a higher level. We are at a Level 1... a work camp. Work camps are for the least violent and least dangerous criminals with the shortest sentences. If you have a longer sentence, you go to a Level 2 or 3, or even 4 or 5. Edgar's job at the higher-lever prison was in the shoe shop. He earned extra money off the records by resoling gym shoes. He said that people who had been in jail for five or ten years paid him $5 per pair to resole their shoes, rather than buy new pairs. He said he made about $30 a day "off the books" that way. In January of 1991 they sent him here. In April his judge said he could go to boot camp. Boot camp is six months long, and then you have six months of home arrest. The rest of your sentence time just goes away. Even though the judge recommended him for boot camp, his team did not send away the appropriate paperwork. So Edgar protested to the warden. The warden said, "Tough luck."

I was talking to this old Mexican guy whose only job is to clean two windows in the dorm. He said he was in here for cocaine. Here is his story. His son got arrested and they hired a lawyer. The lawyer asked for some cocaine as part of his fee. The dad went out and bought some cocaine and shipped it to the lawyer. Unfortunately, the lawyer was working for the DEA, and so they busted the dad and now here he is.

Within one month of arriving at prison, I am supposed to get a computation sheet that shows when I get out. They have two days left to get me my sheet. If I don't get it, I'm not sure what I should do. One inmate told me that I should fill out another cop-out sheet. The real title of a cop-out sheet is "Inmate Request to Staff Member."

11-21: I was supposed to check into the hospital at 6:00 a.m. It is now 9:00 a.m., and the hospital is still not open. A guard went inside and found the PA, or physician's assistant, asleep on the floor. He was drunk. He is the head PA for the prison. I don't have too much confidence in the health-care system in here.

I met a drug dealer who told me he had a Porsche stored in a storage shed. When he was out on a furlough, he went to check on it. The storage bin place said that there was a fire there, and that's why his Porsche was no longer there. He said he did not have any insurance on the Porsche. He also said he had a big Scarab boat and left it with a friend at an auto dealer yard. He said that his friend sold the Scarab and left town. The drug dealer seemed fairly bitter about these events. He also said he got a long sentence because he wouldn't snitch on anyone. But the prison officials do not give furloughs to druggies, so he must have snitched on someone. (*Editor's note: This is not true at all federal prison camps.*)

Let me tell you about Randall. He was Cliff's bunkie before me. He is six feet, four inches tall, and real skinny. He has not cut his hair in two years. It is blonde on top and light brown underneath. Randall takes a hair shower in the sink every morning. Cliff, my bunkie, who is the dorm orderly, hates that because Cliff has to clean it up. If you ask Randall a question, there is about a 45-second delay before he begins any sort of answer. At first I thought he did not like to talk. But now I realize that that's just the way he answers.

Yesterday my team paged me and gave me papers saying that I am supposed to appear before the parole board in February. Theoretically, the parole board can release me in June. I know that is for Count One, which is old law. And my second count is new law. They don't seem to have my second count registered here at the prison. The inmates tell me to keep my mouth shut. And they tell me about an inmate who accidentally got let out too early. Everything was going fine for several years, and then the former prisoner asked to move to a different state. At that point, the Bureau of Prisons noticed that they had let him out too early. They made him come back to prison to finish his sentence, but at least the time he was out was counted as time spent in jail, since the BOP made the mistake.

Here is my new schedule:
6:30 a.m. Checkout point Get on a truck. Get to my job by 7:00. Go back for lunch at 10:45. Go back to checkout point at 12:00. Get to my job at 12:30. Lock up to go back by 2:30. That's three and a half hours at my job in the morning and two hours at my job in the afternoon.

My bunkie Cliff showed me his co-defendant, who is here, too. Cliff says he is a snitch. I am beginning to think everybody here is a snitch.

This inmate, Irvin, is trying to switch jobs. He doesn't like his R&G crew, so he went to the clinic and told them he was allergic to bee stings, even though that was not in his medical records. The clinic promised that they would change his crew. That was three days ago. Now Irvin is trying to get his boss to get him transferred.

11-26: Last night a few of the guys had a going away party for Chris, one of the Michael Milken guys. He has been down for 37 months. I was invited because Delmar threw the party. Of course, we ate dip and crackers. Chris is in a single cube, and Delmar gets that cube next. There are only four singles on each side of about forty men. If you have a single cube, automatically you are revered as an authority, since you only get one after you've been here for two or three years.

Cliff and Delmar went to the Commissary to get the supplies for Chris's going-away party. Delmar asked me to come along too, but Cliff recommended that I stay there to guard the cube so that no one would rip it off, since everyone knew that Chris was leaving, and wanted to scavenge it. I felt it was necessary, so I kept vigil. At four a.m., Cliff, who normally sleeps till six, got up to claim Chris's mattress. He got two of Chris's blankets, and also scored a pair of gym shoes. At 5:00, normal wakeup time, I went by Chris's cube and it was stripped clean.

I ran into a Jewish guy named Bart. He is not adjusting well at all. He is very scared and keeps to himself a lot. He got a 37-month sentence and a $7.5 million fine. He was expecting an 18-month sentence and a smaller fine. Ray, an inmate who re-enlisted (second time in prison), told me that he knew Bart on the streets and that they were both in here for the same crime. They were involved with some sort of coin scam. Ray said that they did not deliver all the coins that they sold. Ray said that it was an innocent mistake. Bart has gallstones and was scheduled for surgery. He says the BOP deliberately moved up his surrender date so that he missed all his surgery. He is trying to get it taken care of inside here, but it is taking a lot longer than he expected. He has blood in his urine all the time. He says the doctor is scared that if Bart does not get permission to operate soon, and he starts bleeding real bad, that Bart may die here. Bart says that if he dies here, his heirs can sue the doctor.

11-29: Out of the Jewish fellowship, only a few normally pay their $25-per-month dues. The inmates who actually pay are jealous of the ones who don't pay, and call the nonpayers snitches. Some of the members have suggested that if a member Jew could not pay, then a rich member should have the poor member do their laundry. Then the rich member should pay for the poor one.

All of the inmates thought the Thanksgiving Day dinner food was great. I gave away most of my food. The turkey was not real turkey. It was sort of like pressed meat of some kind wrapped up in tin foil. It had a really metallic taste.

A lot of the inmates in here are making plans for what to do when they get out of federal prison camp. Inmate Ober is getting into bridge this year. He says that when he gets outside, he plans to get into a bridge club. He believes that this is a really good way to meet someone who is rich. Then that someone who is rich can give Inmate Ober a high-paying job. I heard that last year Inmate Ober got into tennis real heavy for the same reason.

There is a Toastmasters Club in here. It meets every other Wednesday from 6:00 p.m. until 8:00 p.m. It is like any Toastmasters Club on the outside. The Toastmasters Club has a lot of power. The Toastmasters hand out passes to go make speeches outside the prison. They hand out sodas at every meeting for good speeches. If you, an inmate, want to give a seminar for the benefit of other inmates, the Toastmasters approve or disapprove your topic. If they approve the topic, then they sponsor the seminar and make sure that inmates show up to participate. Toastmasters also has its own separate bank account, and the inmates can spend the money on soda or food for themselves. Inmates all fight over being an officer of this powerful club.

Bart started to tell me a little about his past. He said that when John F. Kennedy was president, Kennedy sent him over to Kuwait so that Inmate Bart could set up the Kuwaiti monetary system. Inmate Bart also stated that he has blackouts from time to time.

12-02: Inmate Frank approached me at the checkout point and told me that he had received a letter from Milton. Milton was the inmate that my lawyer recommended for me to speak to after my trial. I talked to him about prison camps. Milton had been at this camp before I was sentenced. Milton asked Frank to check on me to be sure that I was OK.

Cliff my bunkmate wants me to give him all my food since I am trying to lose weight.

Today Mr. Spanish-Speaking, one of the Spanish-speaking inmates on my crew, started to talk to me. He said that he used to be a bank officer and he had a six-month trial. He has been down for six years and has been to six different institutions. I found out that Mr. Spanish-Speaking is from South America, and his father is a big coffee exporter. He sent his son to the United States and they bought up a bank. Mr. Spanish-Speaking said that the bigger banks did not like him and therefore they put him in jail. He showed me a newspaper article about himself. It had a picture of Mr. Spanish-Speaking standing beside a Rolls-Royce with his personal jet airplane in the background. He said that when he first got his 15 year sentence he freaked out. He said that he was going through bankruptcy at the time and he had a paid-off $2 million house.

Since it was his personal home, Mr. Spanish-Speaking felt certain that he could keep it despite the bankruptcy. After he lost his trial, his lawyer told him that he should sell the house so that the judge wouldn't hate him so much. Mr. Spanish-Speaking gave his lawyer power of attorney to sell the home. The lawyer sold it in two days and kept the money. Then, to top it off, Mr. Spanish-Speaking got the maximum sentence from his judge anyway.

He says that when he first went to prison, he was in a higher-level one, and the Bureau of Prisons has a special suicide squad assigned to new inmates who come in. The suicide squad tries to acclimate the inmate to his new surroundings and make sure that he doesn't kill himself.

A lot of inmates say that the holidays are hard for them, because that is when they miss their families the most.

Delmar has now decided that he wants to be Jewish. He asked me to help him to get into the club. We figured out that his grandmother was Jewish on his mother's side, so technically, he is Jewish. He will be eligible for the special food and off-camp visits on Friday nights.

Delmar believes that there are a lot of rich people here in this camp. I don't think that is true. I just think that the inmates like to tell a lot of lies since it is Camp Wannabee.

12-03: All of the inmates are getting crankier and crankier the closer we get to Christmas. I hear that this grouchiness lasts through the New Year.

Jeremy, my boss, stopped by my job site. I asked him if he could get me some hot tea. He said that he would get me something, but I would have to hide it in the woods, and be careful.

12-04: The military guys came and dumped an office desk in the woods. Jeremy (my boss) said that I should smash it with a sledgehammer. I took the bulldozer and smashed it. It was an adventure.

Monroe, the inmate who has a brand-new infant child even though he has been down for two years, is 29 years old and has been married for nine years. His wife was 15 years old when he married her.

Last night a new celebrity came into camp. He is one of the Ivan Boesky guys. I went to talk to him, and he was worried about getting raped. He told me that his family was coming for a visit Saturday and that they were flying in their own family jet plane. He said that he picked this prison camp because he wanted to play tennis. He said that Michael Milken is having a hard time in prison because he can't wear his toupee.

Mr. Boesky Guy is arrogant. He says he has two kids and runs his family in a traditional way, meaning that he tells his wife what she can and cannot do. He says that he needs to get a place near here and supply it with three automobiles, so that when his family flies in, they and the airplane captain will have enough cars to get around.

Later, when I saw Mr. Boesky Guy with his family in the visiting room, his wife told me that a friend with a small Cessna airplane (not a jet) graciously flew them here for their first visit. After that, she said that she will have to drive by herself with their children. Mr. Boesky Guy also said that there was a hit man out to get him.

Delmar stopped by my job site. He brought me some fruit. Snake was telling me that Delmar works where the prison guards cannot go. So several weeks ago, when the hacks raided all the R&G shacks, Delmar's crew was not touched. Delmar works for some big officer on the military base. He keeps the officer's lawn at his personal residence clean.

I understand that at the higher-level prisons, you do not have to work. Prisoners there are considered to be at a prison, not at a work camp. The prisoners at the higher levels have much more time for themselves, but the violence is far worse.

2-05: Once a week, we get safety tips and have to sign off on a sheet that we understood the tip. This week's tip is to check the oil in the machinery, because if you do, the machine will run better. I signed off on it.

SIX MONTHS INTO THE SYSTEM

4-13: I found out this morning that they are going to put me on the Silver Bullet to transfer me to another prison camp. This is the first time I will have to be handcuffed and get Diesel Therapy on the bus.

I went to report to R&D, and the guard there gave me five boxes to pack up my stuff. After I packed up all my stuff, I had to give the boxes back to R&D. The boxes are mailed to my new camp, not put on the Silver Bullet with me. After that I had to go around to all of the departments (like laundry, and the rest) and have them sign off on my Pre-Release Clearance Schedule. The Schedule must be signed off by several departments such as cashier, hospital, clothing room, R&D, and your case manager.

Kent across the hall asked me for my mattress. Mr. Boesky Guy said he knew somebody that was at my new camp and was already getting a furlough. He also said my new camp gives six-months' halfway house to everyone.

I had to bring my bed-board back to the hospital. Now I have to go back to R&D and turn in my form. Jeb said he heard I was being shipped to Minnesota and Colorado. He asked me which rumor was true. Les said that his son, who is at my new camp, hates it because there is nothing to do at night. But the visiting room is better. Who knows what is true? Some people said they heard that I am going to Atlanta. Atlanta is considered a very bad prison for inmates.

4-14: Joey, my spades-playing partner, had breakfast with me. At 6 a.m. I walked up to control with Wallace and went into R&D. The hack there took my clothing and gave me bus clothing, which is basically a pullover shirt and pants. I brought a book up there with me and I am glad I did because the bus didn't pull in until 8:00. The marshalls came in and put a chain around my waist and handcuffed my hands to it. The marshalls asked me if I was dangerous. I replied, "Not that I know of," and told them that this was the first time I was ever handcuffed. In return, they made the attachment to the waist and the handcuffs so loose I could raise my hands above my head. This is very unusual. Generally they cuff your hands very close to your waist and you cannot use the bathroom very well. Then the marshall put the leg irons on me, and we did the Prisoners' Shuffle to the Silver Bullet. The Silver Bullet had all new seats in it. It was like a Greyhound bus. Except for the bars on the windows. The driver was behind an enclosure of bars, and a guard stood right next to him with a shotgun. In the rear there was another guard with a shotgun. That was unnerving. Several of the other inmates on the Silver Bullet asked me to push down their handcuffs, since they could not do it. It was OK for a while, but I wouldn't want to do it for any length of time.

I was strip-searched when I walked into camp, and I was given a bright-red jump suit. After I filled out some forms, the guards took five pictures of me. Then I went to eat. The red jumpsuit broadcasted to every other inmate in camp that I was new. I saw Inmate Melvin, whom I knew from my old camp. We chatted for a while. He said he likes it here. I went to the hospital, and another PA checked me out. I started getting my slips of paper again: extra pillow, lower bunk, soft shoes... they honored everything that my old camp had given me. Inmate Melvin said that at this camp, all the good jobs are out on the military base and an inmate has to fill out a cop-out sheet to get one.

The R&D guard asked me tax questions. He said that he owed the IRS for back taxes, and asked me what he should do about it.

Here the dorms have rooms with doors on them. Each room is about twenty feet by fourteen feet. The sleeping rooms have carpet on the floor. Eight inmates go in each room. At first the administration assigned me a bed, but it was still occupied. So they gave me another one.

Inmate Melvin says there are only eight Jews here because there are no special benefits. This camp allows visits on Friday nights for everyone.

I went to the Commissary tonight to get some things, and my account had not been transferred as I had been promised.

The guy who sleeps above me, H.L., told me that the reason the inmates want to work on the military base is for the food. On the base, the inmates are allowed to eat lunch with the military people, and they get to eat as much as they want. Another inmate came into the room and said he was just hauled into the Lieutenant's office because he blew a kiss at a woman staff member.

4-15: I went to an A&O meeting all day, and it was basically the same as it was at my old camp. The administration had someone from each department come in and feed us a line of crap. The medical person told us all about AIDS; the financial person said we (the inmates) have to pay our fines. At lunch I went to R&D to pick up my boxes. The hack again talked taxes with me. Of course, this FPC has different rules, so I had to send back some stuff and I could have brought in more of certain things.

At this camp, there is no paging system, so if you leave your dorm, you have to sign in and out every time so that the administration can find you whenever they need to. If you do not do this, and they come looking for you, they will write you up for not signing out.

At A&O, they stressed that inmates should shower every day. Inmate Melvin introduced me to Les' son. Les was my bridge partner at my old prison. Les' son's name is Frank, and he wanted to hear how his dad was doing.

It is nice not having a PA system, because it is less noisy. I hear that on Saturday nights, they show movies to the inmates.

My bunkie Philip was a savings-and-loan owner from Houston. Philip said he paid seven or eight times capital for the banks he bought. I had always heard that they go for five times capital.

4-16: At this prison, there are no "beeps" on the phone when I call. The prison population here seems older.

At this camp, there is an inmate rabbi. Levy is his name. He said he could get me a job anywhere I wanted. He told me that if I wanted to work in the kitchen, I should lie to the guards and tell them that I worked in the kitchen before. Levy said the dish room job was about a two-hour-a-day job. That sounds good to me. But Levy is an inmate. So what he told me could easily be a lie.

The inmate rumor mills tell me that they are going to get a new phone system here. In the new system, the phone calls are to be paid by the inmate's commissary account. The new system is supposed to be in place by September. (Later, I found out that this whole new phone system thing was just an inmate rumor and was totally untrue.)

4-17: At this prison camp, the inmates keep their lights on late at night. At my old camp, they had to turn the lights off at a certain time. At night about half of my room (four out of the eight guys) make the famous Inmate Dip, except here they make it with a variety of cheeses.

I asked Inmate Small about his job as van driver. He said that an inmate had to be one year short to get that job. This means that you have to have only one year to go on your sentence. The inmate van driver cannot have any family in the area, and he must have obtained community custody. Small said that there were two drivers for the medical staff, and one town driver. Small was the medical driver, but the town driver was leaving in three weeks. Small said I should talk to my counselor about it.

My counselor, according to the inmates, is supposed to be a good one. I am scheduled to introduce myself to her on Sunday, so I will ask her about the job. If I don't get that van driver job, I would like a training-center job. I probably will not get either one, but what the hell. I might as well ask.

Remember that Preston promised to introduce me to the administrator who hires in the kitchen? Well, I saw Preston in the kitchen, and he did not introduce me to the administrator who hires the inmates there as he promised that he would.

Bart, one of my roommates, was a dope dealer. He is an older man with a gray beard. Bart said that in addition to running dope, he ran a phone-answering service. Bart says when he gets out, he will set up an answering system again, and he will franchise his system all over the country.

Every inmate has his when-I-get-out story. Several of the inmates have come and asked me to look over their prospectus for their latest money-making schemes. Theoretically, they are not allowed to write these business plans in prison, but everybody does it anyway. Prison is where I first heard about ostrich farming. Every inmate knows that he will get rich doing ostrich farming once he gets out.

It is 7:15 p.m. I ran into Officer Richman, who told me he wanted me to clean up the training center. So I went and got some supplies and went to Control. After I had waited for about thirty minutes, Richman finally showed up and took me to the training center. I asked Richman to come back in a half hour because I had to call you. An hour and a half later, he showed up to get me. As I was riding around in the van, the inmates were staring at me. Richman dropped me off at the phones. More stares. I went back to the dorms. But I missed mail call. Now I will have to stay up till 9:00 to get my mail. Watch. I probably won't even get the job that I want.

Here, the hacks eat with the inmates. At my old camp, the two stayed apart.

The computer guy works in the library. He said he would save me the Sunday newspapers. I asked the computer guy if I could cut out certain articles and send them to you. He said if I come over to the library, he has a razor so that I could cut out the articles. Having a razor is strictly forbidden, of course.

A little while ago, in my room, two inmates were friends. They got into a fight, so both of them were shipped.

At 7:00 tonight I have an ear test/hearing appointment. It is my first hearing appointment. I have not had an eye exam or tooth exam since I got into the prison system.

I was doing my laundry in the laundry room and an inmate laundry man offered to help me. I wonder what laundry costs here.

I have a meeting with the shrink. Someone here told me not to look at her legs. They say she wears short skirts, and if an inmate looks at her legs, she asks the inmate if he has a sexual problem. Who doesn't have a sexual problem in prison?

After my visitors left, I was strip-searched. The guard put his hands in the pockets of my pants, had me take off my socks and my shorts, and had me lift up my private parts. The guard said I could not keep the pants without any pockets. When I turned in my modified pants to the guard on my floor, he asked, "What were you doing, playing pocket pool?" I just said, "No, I just wanted to make sure I didn't keep any change in my pockets when I left the visiting room."

Also, when I was leaving the visiting room, I noticed another inmate threw something to an inmate walking along the road that surrounds the visiting area. It turned out to be cigars. I guess his guest brought a bunch of them to their visit, and the inmate is sharing them with a pal.

Here's a new inmate rumor. I hear that the BOP is going to expand halfway house to ten months. That would be great. According to Bart, the ex-drug, library, roommate, the new policy is supposed to take effect in May. Everyone is excited. There are always rumors like this running rampant among the inmate population. I hope this one is true, but most of them are not true at all.

4-20: I went to see the shrink. She is an older person, and not attractive at all. I told her I get depressed because I miss my family. She said that was normal, and did I want to join one of the group therapy sessions she was running? I replied that whatever she wanted to do would be fine with me. She said she would evaluate me next week. I am not so sure whether group therapy would be good or not. I would not feel comfortable talking to inmates about being lonely for my family.

I asked my roommate Bart for more proof on the ten-months halfway house rumor. I want to believe that it is true. He claimed that if I wanted to see it in writing, I would have to read several different sheets. He said it was not on only one page or in one area. I gave up. I'm losing hope. I guess he made up the whole story.

Jeremy, one of the other roommates, was caught smuggling in amino acids. Amino acids are some sort of weight lifters' pill. He got a "shot," which means he was written up by the guards for doing something wrong. He had to do some extra duty, and he is not allowed out on the base for six months. Jeremy claims that all of the inmates have amino acid pills, but the administration only put the screws to him. That is probably true.

Exciting news: The kitchen here serves jalapeno peppers. So I can eat them in salads or on a sandwich.

Reverend Henson, a chaplain here, said that today was his last day. He said that he knew that I was being transferred from my old camp one week before I was actually transferred. What a liar. He says that the inmates told him that I was transferred because I was a troublemaker. At one point

Henson said, "You look like you're not getting any sleep." Then he asked me a lot of other questions. Henson told his secretary to pull up all the messages pertaining to the day I was transferred to see why I was transferred. Henson was very obviously looking for information. So I gave him none. I wonder why he was so curious. He was probably trying to shake me down for money or something. I don't trust anybody.

It started to rain, so I went to see my counselor, Miss Gold. She told me I was supposed to fill out a visitor list. I told her I already prepared my visitor list when I was at my old camp. She jumped all over me with both feet. She later apologized, and said that it was a hectic day and I should come back tomorrow at 5:00 and just leave her alone today. The inmates said that Counselor Gold was very moody. One day she is real nice and the next day she is nasty.

4-21: I have decided to try to lose some weight. One of the things I am going to do is give up breakfast. Frank, one of my roommates, wants me to give my breakfast to him. He woke me up, anxiously asking, "Is this the day I get your breakfast?"

Last night my bunkie Philip was trying to project the image that he is still a rich man. He said that when he gets out he is going to take a six-month excursion on his 42' ketch. I also overheard him telling someone else that he has 180 acres in Texas somewhere. I notice that he has no extra food in his locker and uses the BOP shampoo instead of buying his own at the commissary. Philip is probably one of those "rich guys" with no money in his commissary account. Something doesn't add up. Philip also said that most of his business contacts stated that they will do business with him when he gets out.

Chaplain Henson said that Chaplain Woodyard is still being investigated by the grand jury. It is supposed to meet again next month.

I went to the visiting room at night and there were only six or eight inmates playing cards, not like at my old camp where you had 50. Here, a lot of the inmates play cards in their rooms.

I saw the doctor today and he just rewrote all of the medical stuff I had before. I had a slip for the following items: (1) 20-pound weight restriction (2) soft shoes, (3) second pillow, (4) extra socks (5) lower bunk, (6) bed board. Now I have those same slips again. Tonight at the commissary I am purchasing two Bic pens, one shoelace, daily vitamins, and three boxes of Kleenex. I decided not to get any ice cream or candy.

When I was seeing the doctor, he told me that once he had to write a slip so that an inmate could wear a sock on his penis. It was something about a venereal disease. The inmate with the sock on his penis has already gone home. The doctor said that the guards were always sending this inmate to the hospital because he wore a sock on his dick.

Jermaine asked if I had heard that all the old law people were getting shipped to Eglin or Maxwell because the parole board only visits those camps. Jeremy said that he was glad to hear that those inmates were getting out of here, because he was sick of hearing them cry about how they had to do two-thirds of their sentence. Jeremy said that we new law people had to do 85% of our sentences.

Today there is a town meeting. That is where the administration calls all of the inmates together, and they talk to us. They said that everyone who has to go up in front of the parole board (old law) has to go to Eglin or Maxwell. I guess the rumor was true.

4-22: My roommate Jermaine said that Officer Richman, Team Person Gray, and the Super in charge of the training center all told Officer Larson to give me the job at the training center. Jermaine says I should get it. Let's see if that is true. You know how much I believe inmates.

I was granted Community Custody at the Team meeting. I am thinking maybe now I can become a town driver.

4-23: Kermit, one of my other roommates, is 31, married, with a two year old daughter. Kermit was caught with two ounces of cocaine, and received a one-year sentence. I guess Kermit must have rolled over on a bunch of people.

I am going down to talk to Lieutenant Adams today to see if he will give me the town driver job. That would be a nice job because I could drive around and see a little of the real world.

I am eating breakfast with Frank again, or, actually, Frank is eating my breakfast again. Frank said that he was involved in a forgery ring. He said that the state busted him first. He pleaded out and got state probation. Then the feds charged him with another charge and he pleaded out to that one. But this time he landed in jail.

Let me see, out of the eight people in the room, Jeremy, Bart, Jermaine, Kermit, and T.J. are druggies. Frank is a forger, and Philip is an S&L guy. T.J. is 21; Kermit is 31; Bart looks 55 or 60; Jeremy looks 35; Frank is 29; Jermaine looks 40.

I had a dentist appointment at 9:00. The dentist said my teeth were good. I asked if he could clean them for me. He and the hygienist both agreed that my teeth were in good shape and don't need to be cleaned. The dentist stated that a healthy person only needs his teeth cleaned every twelve to eighteen months.

I was in line to get a blood test, and the PA who drew blood from the inmate in front of me sliced the inmate's vein, and the inmate was bleeding like a stuck pig. All the inmates still in line for blood drawing, including me, were scared to death. When my turn came up, he didn't slice my vein, but I had a bruise for a week.

4-24: I saw Lieutenant Adams at about 5:00 p.m. He brought me into his office and said that he was looking for someone who could say no to temptation and could say no to an inmate who asked him to do wrong. Adams said he had already filled the current position, but if I would put in a cop-out maybe I would get the next opening. Adams was just giving me a big line of bullshit. He had no intention whatsoever of giving me that job. And I had no intention of talking to him.

4-25: I hate the TV in our room. The other inmates think that if it is the weekend, they are supposed to stay up late, so they blare the TV all night. I hope we do not get it again for a while. If my room does not have the TV, it is easier for me to sleep at night.

Most of the inmates in the room are down watching the softball game. The inmates are playing against the military. The gambling is heavy. Jeremy said that the military people had bet thousands of dollars, and Jermaine was trying to get into the action. They bet on the TV sports here too, just like they do at every prison camp.

4-26: The prison softball team beat the military softball team by ten runs. The inmates were very happy and they partied all night.

Bart the librarian is trying to set up a business with Philip when they get out.

4-27: Well, it is almost May. Another month down. I know we got them by the balls now. Or so the saying goes.

I went over to the commissary to buy some stamps, and my money had still not arrived. We received ten or twenty new inmates today. Rumor has it that the administration will take one TV room from each floor and make it into sleeping quarters, because of our overcrowded status. Update: The camp absorbed the new inmates, and the administration did not take away any TV rooms yet.

4-28: I could not get to sleep last night and today I am exhausted. This room sleeps all day and parties all night.

Jeremy was talking about his bet on the inmate softball teams. He also boasted that the government was after him and he had three houses. The government took one of the houses as a forfeiture. Jeremy sold another house for $125,000. The government froze the money from the house sale, so Jeremy made a deal with the government so they released the money from the one house and Jeremy got to keep both that money and his last house that he still has in a resort area in Colorado. All this from a guy who "did not snitch on anybody." Yeah, right. Every inmate gets the government to release $125,000 once they have their hands on it.

T.J., the 21-year-old, says he was arrested in September of 1990. He pleaded out and was allowed to roam around the streets for a year and three months. Now why would the government allow that? Could it be that he was entrapping other people?

Maurice said he has been in prison since 1986, which is not a good thought. Maurice asked how much time I received. I replied, "Too much." Maurice said, "Well, we all got too much." I replied, "I didn't get as much as you," and left it at that.

At about 12:00 noon, Mr. Larson, who is in charge of the A&Os, calls out "Sharp!" I was reading a book waiting for the A&O officer. I looked up and he signaled me to follow him. I followed Larson to his office. He did not say one word to me. We got into his office and he asked, "What's the name of the IRS lady who is auditing your records?"

He caught me off guard, and I didn't know what he meant. So I asked, "What lady?"

Larson snapped, "You know!"

I said, "Let me go back and get her letter and I will tell you her name."

Larson grabbed a phone message slip from his desk with her name and number on it. He picked up the phone and dialed the IRS lady's number. Then he handed me the phone. Larson was allowing me to use the telephone in his office that is not monitored and recorded. Why would he do that? I was nervous. Evidently the IRS gets special privileges. I took the phone from Larson and the IRS lady said that she would like to meet with me at the prison. I replied that I had already sent her a letter and that she should get it on Wednesday. I said to her that I requested a certain form and her manager's name. She continued talking, trying to justify why she had sent her prior letter to me about not wanting to come to my old prison camp to see me. She seemed worried. She kept talking and talking. I could barely get a word in edgewise.

Finally I said that getting the records was a problem for my wife because they were all in storage. And then I said that since I was under the direction of the government, and that since she worked for the government, that I was sure that she could get me a legal furlough so that I could go to get her the records. She went on and on again about how she would meet me at my new prison, but that going to my old prison had been just too far for her to travel. When I finished with her, Larson told me that he wanted to talk to the IRS lady by himself, and he told me to leave. God only knows what he said. The whole time I was talking to the IRS lady, Larson was listening in.

Ever since I lost my trial, the IRS started auditing our tax returns for every open year. Even after I got to prison, they continued to harass me. At one point, they wanted to have me meet them outside of the prison. I told them that I was in prison and couldn't get out. They wrote me a letter and gave me two separate dates to get out of the prison walls and meet with them. I wrote back and told them that I wouldn't be released by those dates, so there was no way I could get out and meet with them. After the two dates had passed, the IRS wrote back to me and said that since I decided not to show up for those meetings, they would rule against me.

I met with the shrink again. She said that I should try to get into one of her therapy groups to develop trust with other inmates. I thought that would be a cold day in hell, but I agreed to her proposal. The shrink has three groups, and she said she would try to get me into the smallest group, the Tuesday group. The shrink said that this was the most supportive group. She said that the three groups have a total of about thirty inmates in them. That represents over ten percent of the inmate population. It sounded quite high to me. I should have figured out that these programs were a popular thing among inmates. I should have gotten involved with them. But I guess I was dense. The shrink told me that the Wednesday group was the most chaotic. Anyway, I thought I would just go and listen and not say anything, and that way I would not get into trouble.

The shrink informed me that the Tuesday group is currently talking about woman problems: girlfriends or wives and the problems associated with them. She said that before that the group session talked about the problems they were having with the military bosses. And before that they talked for some time about worry or guilt or something. This basically sounded like a waste of time. Also, since she told me all about what was being discussed, I guess whatever you say at group therapy is not in confidence. It is public information. None of this gave me any sort of level of comfortability.

I got a job. It is captain's orderly. That basically means I stay in camp and get ordered around by the captain.

I have to leave my room now because a guard is searching it.

4-29: I have changed my morning schedule again. This time I changed it in hopes of getting into the shower BEFORE the hot water runs out.

Last night a guard came and packed up all of my bunkie Philip's stuff out of his locker. The other inmates in the room believe that if they leave his bed made, the administration will not notice that he has left, and will not reassign his bunk.

At my job I went around to several offices emptying trash, and a small guy named Freeman said that at 11:30 a.m. I would have to come back and empty the trash in the warden's three offices. Next, this inmate named Irvin said I would have to do the mail every day. At this point I got the idea that all the other inmates were giving me the jobs they hate. Well, I was the new inmate on the job, and shit rolls downhill.

Olan is one of the eight people on my crew. Olan says he hates it here. And he hates all the other Jews. Olan also hates Frank, Les' son. Olan said that he is trying to get transferred to my old camp. He said that he has been here for about three months.

I went to get the mail, and the lady who was in charge of it asked if I have any lifting restrictions. I replied yes. She said, "Well you can do the mail today anyway, but you will not be able to do the mail any more." I replied, patriotically, of course, that I would be willing to do any job that the administration has for me with or without any weight restriction. We went to the mail room, picked up the mail, and brought it to the mail room on the first floor of the building. After that I walked around the block for about twenty more minutes and then went in to see if anyone else wanted me to take out the trash. A few officers did, and then Mr. Ted told me to vacuum a rug. I did the vacuuming, and then some other guard told me to take some trays over to the kitchen. Then a small black inmate said to get lost. He said go over to the library until lunch, so here I am.

The other inmates said that our crew is allowed to go into the TV room, but we should not be caught in our dorm rooms, because we are supposed to be working.

Olan came from a higher-level prison, as did Olan's friends. And they like to sit around bitching about this place. One gripe is that the warden is terrible because he never comes in. Apparently this warden was the warden at Atlanta when the Cubans took over a while ago. After that the BOP transferred the warden here. These inmates also did not like the fact that every hack makes up his own rules. Apparently inmates who come from a higher-level institution have a hard time adjusting to a Level 1 prison camp.

There are five inmates on my crew, and three of them are leaving soon. Olan is trying to get transferred. Freeman is due to leave the early part of June. The fifth guy, according to the other inmates, is an asshole. I saw him briefly. His job is to wash the two downstairs doors and vacuum the two throw rugs in the hall and sweep the landings. It seems that he does that first thing in the morning and then does nothing for the rest of the day. This pisses the other inmates off, so they hate him. Freeman told him he would have to do the mail, and this guy decided to scream and yell at Freeman, calling him a snitch.

Bart says the guard in the clothing room hates everybody. He says he can't get another shirt. He has only three shirts because someone stole his fourth one, and the guard keeps telling him that the federal prison camp does not have any more shirts in his size. Bart also showed me a trick. He took some of the perfume ads in the magazines, the ones with the smells on them, and he put them in his pillow. He says it gives them a decent smell.

4-30: This morning I cleaned out The Hole. The Hole is where they send problem inmates. There are two beds or one bunk bed, a combination toilet/sink/water fountain, and that's all. I had to take out all the laundry, and turn the mattress, and put disinfectant on it. Then I had to clean the potty and mop the floors.

Then I went back to my room and got a book and started to leave. Officer Ted saw me and said I was not supposed to work with a book. I just went back into the room and left the book. Then I went over to the library and checked out a book over there.

I went back to get my clothing out of the dryer. This fifth captain's orderly was taking out my clothing. The trouble was, my clothes were not dry yet. He said, "Tough shit." I put my clothes back in anyway. I went back to the room and Jermaine said that I should take Philip's locker with the extra pockets. I paid Jermaine two packs of smokes and a six-pack of soda for shelves for my locker, and Jermaine just says "Take Philip's."

My job seems to consist of a little work and then a lot of hiding. Hide, come back, make sure everybody knows you are around, and then hide again. The hiding gets difficult. Nobody has anything to do.

5-01: It is 6:55 a.m. Last night an inmate came in. I didn't catch his name. He was babbling on and on about nothing. Jeremy said to the new guy, "How high are you?" He evidently got high before he reported to camp.

I heard from an inmate that I would probably not be on my job long. The administration gives that job to people who have gotten into minor trouble so that they can watch them closely. Minor offenses include talking on the outside telephones, or smuggling in minor things from the base. So Bart said I would probably get bumped off the squad. Bart said that when he gets out of prison, he will continue to do illegal things. He said it is a way of life for him.

Olan said that the BOP was planning to close Tyndall, and that they are going to build a new dorm at Saufley, and all the people at Tyndall are going to get transferred into Saufley.

Olan said that we were allowed to eat in the honored short line because we were captain's orderlies. The short line is for all the kitchen help. They eat before everybody else does, and after they are done eating, then the general population eats.

How To Survive Federal Prison Camp

130

Olan also said we get paid $18 per month instead of the $12 a month that the general population gets.

Anyway, we ate early. It was fried chicken. Olan ate three pieces. At lunch Melvin sat down with us. He works in the kitchen. Melvin asked if I knew his codefendant, Frank Silverberg. Frank was one of the inmates who never, and I mean never, spoke to me. So I told Melvin that I knew him. Melvin said that Frank was facing ten years and he snitched on someone to get his sentence reduced to five. I asked Melvin how much time he got, and he replied, "Two years." I did not ask the next logical question.

Melvin proceeded to tell me his whole life story. His son is a paranoid schizophrenic. Melvin then brought out more chicken for me and Olan at no charge. Melvin said he never charges for extra food. He said he was in the rag business on the street.

Olan started to talk about his background, too. He said he is rich. And he said that he still owns the largest escort service in Florida. I guess that was supposed to impress me. Then Olan asked me if he could borrow $2.

I went up to the dorm and I saw somebody in Philip's bed. He is a new inmate named Bart, and he came straight from the county jail, where he said he spent seven months. Bart has a 46-month sentence for bank robbery.

I went to play cards out by the visiting room. Olan right away growled, "Did Melvin give you any more chicken?"

I said, "What chicken?"

Olan said, "Did Melvin give you any chicken?"

I said, "Melvin is my partner and I am not saying anything."

Then Melvin snarled, "Yeah, I gave him another piece of chicken."

Well, Olan snapped back, "That extra chicken should have been mine. Clive did not have any right to get any more chicken!"

About this time, everybody had to leave the bridge game to go over to the baseball diamond for a natural-disaster preparedness drill. Inmates made two single-file rows, and the guards counted 89 inmates in that section. The other gathering spot for disasters is the tennis courts. At the drill spot, they did the count, which took an hour to clear.

Then the four of us went over to the inside of the visiting room to play some bridge. Olan refused to play because he wanted more chicken. So the other three of us played three-handed bridge.

I was surprised by Olan's pissing and moaning over one piece of chicken. After all, he got three pieces of chicken at lunch. Later, when I was in my dorm room, Olan rushed in, looked at me, and said, "Just checking to see if you are eating chicken." He wasn't kidding. I guess I just made my first enemy here.

After the four o'clock count, all the guards were standing around outside. The inmates say that the administration is keeping extra people around because the administration is afraid of a riot due to the fact that the officers were acquitted on the Rodney King verdict. I really never thought about it, but maybe the guards are correct. Frank and Jermaine saw the extra guards and said, "Let's burn down the place."

Here, a Friday night temple service is run by an inmate named Biff. He has re-enlisted — this is his second trip to prison. And according to the other inmates, if anybody says they know something about anything, then Biff claims that he knows more. Melvin says Biff has sworn that he is a doctor, a lawyer, a chiropractor, owner of a video store, international banker, drug smuggler, and anything else that sounds interesting.

I am helping my new bunkie Bart with his visitor list. He had trouble spelling "sister". I asked Bart if he ever finished high school, and he said no. I told him the administration would probably make him get his GED. Bart replied, "Fuck them."

Bart told me how he ended up here. He went to rob a bank with a note. He handed the note to the teller and they gave him $1,300. The surveillance camera got a picture of him at the bank. On the nightly news they ran a story on the bank robbery and broadcast his picture. Since Bart had robbed the bank in the town he grew up in, everybody called the police to turn him in. He says he robbed a local bank because he didn't feel like driving to a different city where nobody knew him. Bart is 27 years old with a two-year-old child.

Jermaine started telling everybody he could that the administration is ready for a riot. I believe that Jermaine works for the administration here, and they have told Jermaine to spread the rumor so that the inmates know that the hacks are ready for them in case they do decide to riot.

5-2: Last night everybody in the room made a large bucket of "dip" and I had several helpings.

5-3: I heard that guard Knapp, who had visiting-room duty, was watching a basketball game on the TV in the visiting room. An inmate's visiting spouse asked Knapp if he would please change it to cartoons for the kids to watch. Knapp didn't want to change the channel, and became very pissed when the spouse asked him to change it. He changed the rules on what you can bring into the visiting room. You can no longer bring in toys for children at all.

Knapp pulled me out of the count in the chapel to tell me to wash up the chalk on the sidewalk that our kids drew pictures on during their visit. He was mad, even though the outside officer said nothing to us when we were making the drawings. Knapp further told me not to let the kids play in the bushes, because if they got hurt he didn't want to do the paperwork. Also, Knapp told me that our kids could not put two chairs together to make a bed so that they could take a nap. He said that if our kids got hurt, there was too much paperwork to fill out. I can't wait until July when the administration rotates the guards.

Several inmates have approached me and told me that I should file papers against Knapp for making me clean up the sidewalk.

After the visit, Olan, "Mr. Rich Man," hit me up for another sixty-cent loan.

5-4: Jermaine asked me if I had any crackers for his dip. I said yes, and gave him some Townhouse crackers. All of the other inmates in the room went nuts because the commissary here does not sell Townhouse crackers. Needless to say, the crackers were eaten fast.

My new bunkie Bart wants me to buy him some cigarettes, and he said he would pay me back. I'll buy him some, but not a lot. Update: he did pay me back.

I came into my room and caught Jeremy telling everybody in the room that all I did since I got here was complain.

Quite a few of the inmates in the compound are talking about the sailboats we drew in chalk on the visiting-room yard's sidewalk.

In the hall I passed three inmates talking. Two inmates were saying to the third, "Well, what does Jesus our Savior say?" The third inmate walked away. As he went, the two other Jesus guys remarked that if more people accepted Jesus as our savior, maybe not so many people would be in here. In every prison, there are a lot of inmates who have "found Jesus." At some prisons, a lot of the inmates found the Jewish God due to the food.

I saw Olan again and he griped about the chicken.

The tailor brought my shorts back and charged me $2.

5-5: My bunkie Bart was talking to Roger the new town driver. Roger is gay, and Roger told Bart that if Bart ever has any problems, Bart could always find Roger at 1:00 a.m. in the TV room. Roger then asked Bart to meet him there. I guess this is where gay inmates can meet with each other.

That reminds me: I was out walking with Olan, and our hands accidentally brushed when I wasn't paying attention. Olan said, "Oooh. That made my dick hard." I looked at Olan with surprise. I had not realized that Olan was gay. Later inmate Mr. Ober said that he wondered how long it would take for me to figure out that Olan was homosexual and looking for love. Mr. Ober said that I didn't take too long to realize Olan's motives.

Frank the orderly was called down to the lieutenant's office. Usually the lieutenant calls an inmate down to his office so that the administration can pressure an inmate to snitch out other inmates. Then the inmate makes up some bullshit excuse about why he went to see the lieutenant. When Frank returned to the dorm, his excuse was that the captain was there, and the captain asked Frank all sorts of questions about whether or not Frank felt like hitting someone or whether or not Frank planned to run away. Frank said the captain told him that the inmates had complained to him about Frank's aggressive behavior. My guess is that Frank snitched out everyone he could.

Kermit decided to say that I was too cheap to buy anything from the store. I replied, not cheap, just broke.

I went to Friday night services for the first time. An outside rabbi comes in once a month for services. I sat in the back. The rabbi did not bother to come over to say hello. But he talked a lot about the cruise that he just came back from. The rabbi goes on cruises all the time because he can travel for free as the cruise rabbi. Well, the rabbi tells about the cruise and what does the rabbi talk about but the great food and how much there was to eat. At one point he said that the store on the ship had to sell gold things because nobody on the ship would buy anything made out of silver because it was beneath them. The rabbi's bragging was disgusting. The rabbi went on to say that the Seder that he put on here was better than any other Seder at any other prison. I did not tell them that at some camps the Jews go to the Officers' Club for Seder.

NINETEEN MONTHS INTO THE SYSTEM

5- 8: One week to go till I get to halfway house. The hacks are tormenting me right now. They say that they'll make me sweep the sidewalks for six hours. Then they walk away laughing. One officer says, stop calling him sir. Officer Applebaum keeps on announcing that he wants to take away my halfway house and keep me in prison longer. Yesterday Applebaum brought in some bleach to clean the restrooms. His favorite snitch Delmar gave most of it away or sold it to the laundry inmates so they could use it in their wash. Then Delmar gave me the leftover bottle since I was supposed to clean the bathrooms with it. I noticed later that Officer Applebaum called to the lieutenant and that Officer Applebaum tried to tell the lieutenant that I sold most of the bleach. The lieutenant said that she didn't want to hear about it and she walked away.

Kent, the other CPA, says his eight-year-old daughter is running around telling everybody that he is in jail. It seems she overheard a conversation with her mom and somebody else talking abut prison. Kent said that his wife said that she was thinking of dropping her three kids off at the state family services office and leaving forever. Kent was very upset by this. Kent thinks he can get an emergency three-day furlough if he needs it. Kent says that the head inmate of the kitchen told Kent he could get it for him. Since Kent is new, he believes everything he hears.

I am a nervous wreck.

5-9: You know, since my wet dream a few weeks ago, I have not taken care of myself sexually. I am just waiting for the real thing.

Norman is back. Norman left for the halfway house in February. He had a real easy time here. He had the best job off base and got all his furloughs, and he got six months of halfway house. Norman told me he got a speeding ticket, and that's why they sent him back to prison. Update: later, when I went to the same halfway house, I found out that Norman did not have a driver's license or even permission to drive a car. So when he got the speeding ticket, the officer reported it to the halfway house, which promptly violated him for driving without permission.

5-10: The new inmate Jim got up Saturday morning and banged his locker door real loud. Later, I noticed that several inmates were walking up to Jim's locker and leaving. I walked over there and saw that Jim had left his cigarettes out and the inmates were stealing them.

Maximo, who is supposed to leave about one week after me, lost his six months of halfway house. He is a foreigner. The immigration department has a detainer to deport him. So he will be shipped home after he gets done with prison, but he will not get six months of halfway house. Lots of times foreign inmates are not allowed to stay in the U.S. They are deported. Basically, foreign criminals get Diesel Therapy to the New Orleans prison. They are held there for several months until they are put on an airplane and sent home. They are not allowed halfway house because the government does not want them in the U.S.A.

Well, Delmar, the inmate bathroom cop, has finally figured out that the guards want him to clean the bathroom when I leave. Delmar's job, up to this point, has been to watch me clean the bathroom and then tell the guard whether or not I did a good job. Anyway, Delmar goes to the Physicians Assistant at the medical clinic and gets a pass saying that he is allergic to chemicals. Thus, he cannot work in the bathroom. After I got out of prison, I took to calling Delmar "Mr. Two Names" because at one point, both of us applied for a sales job at the same time, and Delmar surprised me with a brand new name and said he used to be a New York police officer.

I am not going to mention the fact that I am leaving on May 17 to my Tuesday shrink group. My only goal is to get out of here and get back to my family.

Some state representative came to walk through the prison today. The hacks came by and told all of us to look busy for five or ten minutes while the state rep walked through.

I went back up to R&D to pick up some boxes to pack up again, this time to come home. There is a new rumor going around prison. The good part of the rumor is that U.S. Attorney General Janet Reno was interviewed on TV and announced that first-time drug offenders should be released from prison immediately. The bad part of the rumor is that Attorney General Janet Reno announced that all white-collar inmates should rot in jail forever.

5-11: Norman is going to tell me all about the halfway house. There are several interesting rumors about Norman and his codefendant, Hoss. Norman and Hoss used to be best friends. Since Norman's wife has already divorced him, Norman was spending his halfway house weekend passes at Hoss's house. Hoss is still incarcerated here. Norman was staying at Hoss's wife's house, but Norman says he was not sleeping with Hoss's wife. They say that Norman told Hoss's wife all about Hoss's wild life and partying before he came to prison. Hoss's wife heard all about Hoss cheating on her. This made Hoss's wife get real pissed off at Hoss. And now Hoss is pissed off at Norman.

5-12: Well, I had a bad night. I woke up at 3 a.m. and could not get back to sleep. Norman had talked to me and told me some terrible things about halfway house. So in the middle of the night I felt hopeless and depressed. This morning, in the light of day, things do not look so bad. I should have realized that Norman would say bad things about the halfway house because he could not make it there. Norman told me that not even a fast-food joint would hire me, because I was a convicted felon. He said I would have a hard time finding any job at all. Now in the daytime I know I can get a job doing something.

Norman said that the halfway house allows you three movements when you went home for the weekend. Each movement would last for three hours. But you could not go to the beach because it did not have a phone. Norman says all you have to do is write down that you are going to the mall and instead you can go where you want. Norman said that everyone lied to the halfway house and went home before work to shave and shower.

Well, today I will have to contend with Officer Applebaum's plan to try to take away my 58 days of halfway house. But I will survive and I will win. I will beat that little son of a bitch and get my halfway house.

At my last shrink group meeting, I was very careful not to say anything about leaving. I don't want any of them to know in advance that I am getting out of here, because I am sure that some of them would try to cause me problems and make me lose my halfway house. For the first time, the shrink sat next to me in the group. As I was leaving the room, she waved goodbye to me. Evidently she knew that I was leaving. I guess Friday I will go over and say goodbye or some kind words. I guess that is what is expected of me.

The shrink said that I should contact her when I get out. She gave me phone numbers to contact her. She is trying to set me up, because this is totally against the rules. The rules say that people who work at the prison are not to have contact with any inmates for two years after they leave the institution. At our last meeting, she said that Roy had called her. And that he was put into a halfway house because the Parole Officer did not approve of the house he was living in. Roy just left here two months ago.

Well, this morning went OK in the restroom. It just so happened that inmate Ortiz had a call-out today, so he helped me with the restroom. Ortiz wants the restroom job, so he is showing off for Officer Applebaum, who is courting him. Everybody is happy, including me. Officer Applebaum is not bothering me.

Kent the CPA said goodbye in the following way: "I wish you would be here next week when I have my team meeting so you could give me advice." Does that mean that he will miss me? I can't wait to get back to a better class of losers.

5-13: Ozzie came back last night. He is all pissed off because he did not get an earlier release date. He stated that even though he won the appeal, based upon erroneous stuff in his PSR, the judge just resentenced him to the same amount of time. Ozzie told me that he owned a large corporation on the outside. From time to time he would show me financial statements and ask me for my opinion on business. I was polite, but I thought he was lying until I read about him in the newspaper after I got out. The paper reported that he had just sold his company for $35 million. I guess he wasn't lying.

Yesterday Sylvester, the president of the bridge club, told me about his crime. Sylvester said he went to law school for about a year and then dropped out. Here is why: What he did was find out which bearer bonds were going to be called. Then he put his OWN ad, with his personal post office box, in the *Wall Street Journal* before the bonds were actually due. His ad stated that the bonds were being called. Sylvester said that people sent their bearer bonds to his post office box.

Meanwhile, he assumed dead peoples' identities, and opened stock brokerage accounts in the dead peoples' names. Sylvester then sold the bonds and transferred the money to gold. Sylvester said that he always left about $100,000 in each brokerage account for the stock broker to "churn" illegally and earn extra commissions. Sylvester said that he looked for bearer bonds that were going to be called by banks that had been bought out by bigger banks. He also always gave the stockbroker power of attorney to trade any way the stockbroker wanted. That way, the stockbroker got his share of the illegal money and never said a word about what Sylvester did.

Sylvester said he got caught because his partner fell in love with this girl who had a boyfriend. The partner wanted the boyfriend out of the picture. So he assumed the boyfriend's identity and used his name. When the FBI came to arrest the boyfriend, the girlfriend ratted out Sylvester's partner, who then ratted out Sylvester. Sylvester said his partner had $2.6 million in bonds in his car at the time of his arrest. Sylvester said that his restitution is $600,000, which he basically owes to Travelers insurance company because they insured the bonds.

Sylvester asked me if he could have some third party offer the insurance company $500,000 for this note. He went so far as to state that he would have it be a foreign corporation that made the offer. Out of all the crimes that I heard about in prison, this was the most clever. A lot of people who have bearer bonds are drug dealers. So Sylvester robbed from people who could not say anything. It was a brilliant plan.

5-14: Last night I waited for the call-out sheet to be posted. And then I saw my name listed for Unit Run. Unit Run means you're leaving. And you have to get checked out by all of the divisions, turn in all your property, and leave. All I could think of was, YES! YES! YES!

Kent the CPA complained that the IRS was telling his clients that he is in jail. That didn't surprise me at all.

Ortiz, the inmate who wants my bathroom job, stayed in yesterday to help. Officer Applebaum went to see Miss Gold to request Ortiz, but she turned him down. Her reason was that he had not been in his job more than six months. This rule is almost never enforced if a guard has asked for you.

Kent the CPA took certain parts of my locker for his locker. Ozzie wants to get my bunk location that I am vacating. At dinner last night, Ron asked me to sit with him, so I did. Ron remarked, "I see you are going home." I replied, "Yes, but please keep it a secret so I don't jinx it." So just as soon as another inmate sat down, Ron blabbed, "Guess what? Clive's going home."

After I called home at around 5:45 p.m. I came out of the phone room and Officer Rex hollered at me. I kept on walking and he kept on screaming that he knew all about the fact that I was leaving and that he let me have my sixty days of halfway house because he was tired of writing me up. Rex was really pissed off that his snitches in my shrink group didn't tell him that I was leaving. He really wanted so bad to take away my halfway house. I felt so good. I beat that bastard!

5-15: An inmate named Earl was caught pissing outdoors. Earl was scheduled to start six months of halfway house in June. Thursday, Earl was put in The Hole, and Friday he was shipped. There goes his halfway house.

I was doing my walkaround, which means that I go to the departments for checkoff to prove that I have returned everything. I had to go to the lieutenant's office for one of the checkoffs. The lieutenant told me to sit down and asked me to tell him which inmates were breaking the laws of the prison. I was taken aback by his question, and he repeated it. I told him I didn't know anybody who was breaking any laws. Then he said, "If you can go out of here with a clear conscience, then go." I said, "Fine," and I left. It surprised me that even when an inmate is leaving, he is pressed one last time to snitch on everybody.

Since I didn't say anything about the fact that I was leaving, inmate rumors are circulating around. They say that I am the first one of the first-time drug offenders to be released by U.S. Attorney General Janet Reno. The Spanish-speaking inmates are waving to me, winking at me, and giving me the thumbs-up sign.

I will need to spend two more days in the bunk, then I will get out of here. I went to tell the shrink goodbye, and she was caught off-guard and forgot to fall into her "I will be happy for you when you leave" mode. She did not say anything like, "I am glad to see you are leaving," or, "Have a good life." I am not sure why that surprised me, since, after all, she is of the human species. The administration people do not give a fuck about you when you are in prison.

There is another town meeting scheduled, and according to the inmate rumors, the administration is going to announce that they will start giving twelve months of halfway house now. Update: I just got back from the town meeting. Unfortunately, what the administration actually announced was that people have been stealing the newspapers, and if it doesn't stop, they'll take away the machines.

Josh, an inmate in my Tuesday shrink group, is furious at me and has refused to speak to me any more. I had heard that Josh was a snitch for Officer Rex. When I didn't announce to my shrink group that I was leaving, Josh couldn't snitch it to Officer Rex. Rex had to learn from the postings on the bulletin board, and now he thinks that Josh is holding out on him. I guess I damaged Josh's credibility with Officer Rex.

Arthur, an inmate that I walk with, had a bomb dropped on him. He was shaving and looked into the mirror and noticed the face of the guy standing next to him at the sink. It was the face of the person that Arthur testified against in court. That person has been assigned to this institution. This is never supposed to happen. The government is supposed to keep inmates who testified against each other in totally separate prisons. This is to save lives. The new inmate has started telling everybody that Arthur testified against him. Arthur went to his counselor to complain, but nothing happened.

5-16: 24 hours to go. I saw a new inmate walking into the bathroom barefooted. I reminded him about shower shoes. You know, I forgot how ignorant new inmates are to the ways of prison.

Earl the pisser came back today. He did not lose any of his halfway house time. Earl said that because he was such a nice guy the administration did not take away any of his halfway house time. Later, Earl was assigned to the same halfway house that I was. I made a phone call when he wanted to use the phone. At the beginning of the phone call, he told me to hang it up or he would kill me. By this time, I was used to it, so I kept on talking. And I am still here to tell about it.

5-17: Well, the day has arrived. Last night while I was eating dinner, Officer Haddock came to me. She said she would like to talk to me before I left, so after I was done eating, I looked her up. She brought me into an office and then gave me a breathalyzer test. I passed. She was furious... really pissed off. I broke out laughing. Here I think she is going to say goodbye and wish me well, but instead the bitch is just trying to make me stay here longer. But I won.

Mr. Ober gave me one last bit of advice: at the halfway house, everyone is a snitch, so beware.

CHAPTER THIRTEEN
RELEASE TO A HALFWAY HOUSE

WHAT NOT TO DO BEFORE YOU ARE RELEASED

This will be a very stressful and scary time for you. You are very nervous because you feel that the hacks would love to keep you in prison. You are not paranoid if you feel that the hacks are plotting against you. They often *are* plotting against you. You are very nervous that you will make one little mistake and end up serving more time. Most of the time you spend at your job, in your bed, or eating your meals. All other free activities stop, as you just try to exist without making any waves until you get released. It doesn't hurt to be paranoid. Not only do the hacks want to get you, but some of the other inmates want to get you, too. Some of them are extremely jealous that you are going to get out and they are not. Many inmates nearing their release date just stay in their bunks as much as possible and emotionally withdraw, trying not to be noticed. After all, this is the time when schemes abound. So it's best not to prance about chirping, "30 days and a wake-up!" and so forth to everyone you encounter.

Instead, play it cool and don't remind everyone of your impending release.

GIVING AWAY YOUR POSSESSIONS

This is not a hard task. The other inmates will come up to you and ask you for the smallest things. One person asked me for a drawer because he didn't like his drawer. The other inmates will fight over who will get your bunk. You might want to give away everything you have. You might not want to have anything to remind you of prison. It is considered top-notch convict behavior to not take anything with you when you leave except your most personal effects.

HALFWAY HOUSE

Now that you have arrived at the halfway house, the first thing that you need to do is get a job. Once you have a job, you can leave the halfway house on weekends to visit your family and friends.

DRIVING A CAR AGAIN

You need to regain your right to drive a vehicle. Your need to drive has to be work-related, and is vehicle-specific. To regain your driving privileges, you have to show your driver's license, title to your car, and proof of insurance. The halfway-house people photocopy all of this information and send it away, and in a week to ten days, you get the right to drive. One rumor said that the halfway-house personnel were going to try to have the prisons do this procedure, but that turned out to be just another inmate rumor.

One inmate can still remember his first time driving a car after he got out of prison camp. He said that the drive was about an hour and a half long, and he felt great. As he drove, he picked up a hitchhiker who was standing beside the road.

Once the rider was comfortably seated in the car, the inmate said to the hitchhiker, "I know how it is to be without a car. Actually, I haven't driven a car for two years."

The hitchhiker's eyes widened. He looked at the inmate, scooted closer to the car door, and asked, "Why?"

The inmate replied, "I just got out of prison."

The hitchhiker gulped once and said, "The next corner is fine, thank you. Just let me out there."

HALFWAY HOUSE REPORTS

During your stay at the halfway house, you will be required to meet with halfway-house personnel to fill out your weekly reports. You will be asked how you are doing at work. You will be asked what you plan to do when you get out. You may be asked if you are saving ten percent of your earnings and if you are having any problems at home. You and the halfway house person will have to sign the weekly report, and it will go into your file.

The halfway-house personnel are often extremely petty, and act inflexibly and "by the book." It's easy to resent this, and begin giving yourself "little permissions" to do unauthorized things, which can result in violation. Don't fall into this trap! Abide by the rules, stupid and condescending as they may be, and eventually you'll be safe at home.

You will not be allowed to socialize outside the halfway house with any other inmate. One time something broke on one inmate's car. One of the other inmates said that he could fix it. The first inmate purchased a part, but when the two asked permission to go to the parking lot to fix the car, the halfway house personnel said that they couldn't leave together because it would constitute socializing outside of the halfway house.

There could be any number of inmates at your halfway house. Some will be women, and some will be men. Only a few of the inmates will attempt to escape.

One resident started a restaurant while he was at the halfway house. He hired two women inmates to be waitresses. He ended up marrying one of the resident-waitresses.

One of the halfway house residents thought that he could serve his whole sentence at the halfway house. He stayed there for eight months awaiting sentencing. At sentencing, he got sent to prison. He said that he felt certain that his halfway-house time would be deducted from his prison sentence. The other inmates knew better, but they didn't have the heart to tell him.

GETTING A JOB

Your first step should be to go to the state unemployment office. There will be one person assigned to helping convicted criminals. You will be sent out on three or four job interviews right away. Take the job that you are offered. You want to get the weekend passes that are given only to those who have worked 40 hours a week. With a job, you will be able to get your first weekend pass, which will happen on the second weekend you are there, and you will get a pass every weekend that you are at the halfway house. You will have to pay the halfway house a percentage of your earnings to defray the cost of your room and board. This will probably be in the neighborhood of 25%.

REPORTING FOR WORK

A representative from the halfway house will come out to your workplace to make sure that your employer knows that you are a criminal. The halfway-house people might call as often as once a week to check up on you.

Generally, travel time to and from work will be dictated by how long is actually necessary to make the trips. You may be given only about 30 minutes to arrive at work after you leave the halfway house, and you will have about 30 minutes to get back to the halfway house after work. You will have to sign in and out noting the time you leave, where you are going, and when you expect to return.

VISITS

The first weekend you are at the halfway house, your family can come there to visit you. It is totally different from a visit in prison. Your visitors are not searched or told what to bring. You should have the TV room to yourself, since most of the other inmates are out of the building on weekend passes. Your guests can bring in street food, which will seem wonderful.

WEEKEND PASSES

On a weekend pass, you actually get to go home for the weekend. You generally have to check in to the halfway house Friday night after work, and then you are released until Sunday around 10:00 p.m. Generally, upon your return to the halfway house at 10:00 p.m., you will be given a breathalyzer test. So be sure that you do not drink alcohol, or, if you foolishly do imbibe, stop drinking at least 24 hours before the breathalyzer, so that alcohol will not be present in your system.

YOUR WEEKEND PASS REQUEST

You must submit your weekend pass request a week before you take it. When on your weekend pass, you are not allowed to leave home except for three three-hour movements or excursions. You have to report these excursions a week in advance, along with telephone numbers where you can be reached during these movements. Obviously, if one of your movements is to a shopping mall, it will be impossible for the halfway house to reach you. You could conceivably go to the beach during your shopping mall time, and no one would be the wiser. But if you do get spotted by a halfway-house staff member who "goes by the book," you could be violated.

The halfway house has the right to call you at any time during your pass. If they do not reach you during their call, you can be sent back to prison. If this happens to you, the halfway house people will send you to the county jail, where you usually sit for two months and then are sent back to federal prison.

CHAPTER FOURTEEN
SUPERVISED RELEASE
(FORMERLY KNOWN AS PAROLE)

Once you make it through your halfway-house time, you will be placed upon supervised release. This used to be known as parole. While you are on supervised release, you have several serious rules to follow. Failure to follow them is a violation of probation, parole, and supervised release, and it could result in an additional prison term for that violation.

YOU HAVE LOST YOUR CIVIL RIGHTS

While you are on supervised release, you are not allowed the right to vote, serve on a jury, or hold public office. The issuance and renewal of some professional licenses such as insurance or real estate licenses are restricted. After your term of supervised release, provided that you have no outstanding criminal charges and you have no outstanding fines from your criminal charges, you can apply for a restoration of your civil rights.

YOU CANNOT POSSESS FIREARMS

Federal law says that persons with felony convictions are forbidden to possess firearms, ammunition, or explosives. At some specified time after the expiration of your supervised release, you can apply for the specific authority to own and possess firearms. Federal law says that once you've obtained restoration of your civil rights, you can apply to federal authorities for the right to own and possess firearms.

YOU PROBABLY CANNOT GET FIDELITY BONDS

Bonding companies usually will not provide a felony bond for a convicted felon. Once a bonding company refuses you a bond in writing, you can apply for the ex-offender bonding program in your state.

YOU HAVE TRAVEL RESTRICTIONS

You may not leave your district without permission of your probation officer. If you need to travel within the continental U.S. and outside your district, you need advance written permission from your probation officer. You need to make these requests at least one week in advance. If your job requires a lot of travel, your probation officer can issue you a blanket pass for the continental United States.

DRUGS ARE PROHIBITED

Any use of illegal drugs during your supervised release may result in violation proceedings against you. Be careful with whom you associate! Even being in the same room with others who are smoking marijuana can result in traces being found in your hair samples and even in your blood stream.

VISITS BY YOUR PROBATION OFFICER

Your probation officer may stop by unannounced at your home or your work site. The officer will ask your employer how your work habits are. The officer will ask for copies of your income tax returns. The officer can require a urine test at any time. However, these urine tests will be more frequent if your conviction included drug charges. You might have several probation officers during your supervised release. You might not even meet the last ones.

Your probation officers will ask you if you told your employer you are a convicted felon. In actual fact, you usually do not need to volunteer any information about your status as a felon to your employers, and probably will never be asked. However, you are not supposed to conceal your felon status from a bonding company, lending institution, licensing agency, or firearms dealer.

YOU SUBMIT A MONTHLY SUPERVISION REPORT

Each month, you must complete and return a monthly supervision report to the U.S. Probation Office. It is due by the 5th of the month. This report is extremely important. If it is not received by the 5th of any month, the Probation Office will violate you for it. The report is the basis for their files.

PHOTOCOPY YOUR REPORTS FOR YOUR FILES

Be sure that you photocopy your reports and follow up by telephone to be sure that they are received. One former convict said that one of his reports was NOT there by the fourth of the month, so he rewrote it and hand-delivered it before the fifth of the month. Perhaps he was paranoid, but he found it hard to believe that it was "lost in the mail." During the last two months he was on probation, he said that he actually hand-delivered all of his reports to the Probation Office in the Federal Building. He didn't want to rely on the mail or anyone else but himself.

Part A of the report asks your name and residence, and if you have moved or if there are any new people living with you.

Part B asks employment information: name and address of employer, position held, did you change jobs and why, is your employer aware you are on supervision, did you miss any days of work, and if you did miss days of work, how many and why.

Part C concerns compliance with conditions of supervision. Were you arrested or even questioned by a law enforcement officer? Did you appear in court for any criminal or even traffic matter? Was anyone in your household arrested or even questioned by a law enforcement officer? Did you associate with anyone with a criminal record? Did you possess or even have access to a firearm? Did you possess or use any illegal drugs? Any "yes" answers must be explained.

Part D deals with your special condition compliance. Do you have a special assessment, fine, or restitution requirement? How much of it did you pay during the month? Do you have any community service work to perform? Attach your monthly schedule of hours worked. Do you have drug, alcohol, or mental health sessions, and if so, how many sessions did you miss?

Part E asks for details about your vehicles.

Part F of the report is your monthly financial statement. You and your spouse must report your income. This must be supported by original pay stubs, which must be attached. Necessary expenses such as home mortgage or rent, groceries, utilities, medical, credit cards, insurance payments, transportation, etc. must be listed for the month. What the probation officer is looking for here is proof that you can support yourself. Because if you cannot prove that you can support yourself, then the probation officer believes that you will supplement your income by committing a crime.

You are asked about the amount of any savings or other financial accounts. You are asked if you filed bankruptcy during the month, and you must list all purchases of individual goods or services on which you spent $500 or more. A warning states that any false statement may result in revocation of probation or parole, in addition to five years' imprisonment, a fine of $250,000, or possibly both. You must use their specially colored original paper forms. You may not submit your report on a white photocopied form.

EXPLAINING VISITS FROM
YOUR PROBATION OFFICER

You can ask your probation officer to act like an old relative when he shows up at your work site. It is embarrassing and distracting to have your probation officer show up at your office, especially if you don't think that your background is anybody else's business.

RANDOM URINE TESTS

At any point, the probation officer can walk through your door and ask you to pee into a bottle. You never know when they are going to show up to ask you to pee. If your case was drug-related, you can expect a pee test every month. As in prison, they have the right to watch as you pee to be sure that it's your own personal urine that they'll be testing. It is degrading, but you've been through worse.

YOU SHOULD AVOID FELONS

You are not allowed to have any contact with any felon without prior permission from your probation officer. Surprisingly enough, even in a new location, you may run into an awful lot of your old prison acquaintances. For example, one time an ex-convict went on a preset sales appointment, and the business owner recognized him from prison.

Another former convict met another ex-convict that he remembered from prison because the second ex-convict was applying for the same job that the first one was trying to get. Except this time, the second ex-convict had a totally new name. The first ex-convict learned from the new boss that "Mr. Two-Names" was formerly a New York cop. If you do not report these incidents, and the other ex-convict does report them, you could be violated and thrown back into prison.

RE-ADJUSTING TO LIFE WITH YOUR FAMILY

At first, there may be problems with control issues in your family. Your wife may be accustomed to making decisions by herself. When you were doing time, she never had to ask you what you wanted for dinner, or when to go to the grocery store. She decided everything, big or small, all by herself for years. Now, suddenly, you reappear on the scene. As for you, after years of no control over your life, you want and need to control. Just keep up the communication, and it will all work out.

In addition, making an appointment with a marriage counselor in order to head off any potential misunderstandings is money well spent. No matter how well-adjusted you think you are, or how happy and easy your expected reemergence in the civilized world is, you should expect some "less smooth" areas in interpersonal relationships. It's a bit like learning how to dance again — your sense of rhythm and that of your partner's may very likely be discordant.

Re-entry, even under the best of circumstances, will not be easy. Make every effort to make your presence comfortable for your partner or spouse.

CHAPTER FIFTEEN
YOU'VE PAID YOUR DEBT

GETTING A JOB AFTER PRISON

You'll find that you are especially qualified for jobs in the sales category. Now that you have gone through the prison system, you have been forced to learn new communicative skills. You probably no longer fear the same things you were afraid of before. You can use this to your advantage in the job market.

Sales jobs pay very well. And the employers are not as concerned about your background. Actually, in prison, the convicts who are auto dealers sometimes hold seminars on how to obtain auto-sales jobs. Auto salesperson is a popular after-prison job, although some states do not allow convicted felons to sell used cars.

ANSWERING QUESTIONS ON JOB APPLICATIONS

Do not answer the question on a job application that asks if you have been convicted of a felony. Just skip that question entirely. You do not want to lie and say you have never been convicted of a felony, because if the employer checks and finds out that you've lied, you're fired. But you don't want to answer "yes" and risk not getting the job in the first place. Just leave the answer blank. If they do ask you directly, you will have to answer honestly. But usually they do not ask. They do not want to know the answer. Of course, your omission will probably be construed as an admission of a conviction, and not an act of principle, if the issue comes up. It's your call.

EXPLAINING BLANKS IN YOUR RESUME

After a term in prison, your resume may seem to have blank spots in the "past employers" section. There will be years during which you evidently held no job at all. Here are two fairly good answers to use in reporting lost time during your career: 1) Say that you decided to retire early, but unfortunately you ran out of money and had to go back to work. 2) Say that you were self-employed during those times. There is another advantage to saying that you were self-employed. Obviously, they will get a glowing reference from a past employer if that past employer was you.

RESTORING YOUR CIVIL RIGHTS

As a convicted felon, you have lost many of your civil rights, and one of those rights is the right to vote. You can apply to have your civil rights given back to you. One ex-convict reports that he decided that he would try to restore his civil rights. He wrote to the Office of Executive Clemency and asked for his voting rights back. A few months later, when he called to follow up, his paperwork had been misplaced. Six months later, they sent him a 15-page application that he had to complete and return within ten days. The application stated that by completing it and signing it, he was giving the government the unconditional right to speak with and question anyone about both his past and his present background. They stated that they specifically planned to question:

- ☐ neighbors
- ☐ employer
- ☐ minister or rabbi
- ☐ ex-wife
- ☐ physicians, hospitals, or clinics
- ☐ school
- ☐ any other person of any kind or character

He was asked to provide his original marriage certificate, all information about previous marriages including marriage licenses and divorce documents, information about his wife's previous marriages including children from that marriage, list of prior residences for the past ten years, what religion he was, name and address of church or temple, original college diplomas, tax returns... the list went on and on. The inmate was totally disgusted. Hadn't he already paid his debt to society? He was really pissed off. He withdrew his application for restoration of his civil rights, and he said to hell with it.

AFTERWORD
BY DONALD B. PARKER

THE "HOLE"

Any convict who passes through a federal prison camp should be aware of the "hole." This is the well-known alternative term for administrative detention or segregation. It is the jail within the prison, the place where convicts who have broken some rule are isolated while their crime is being investigated. For those who didn't experience county jail immediately after their arrest, the hole will be their first real taste of BOP-style incarceration.

Obviously, some people fare better than others in this setting. If you're claustrophobic, you're not going to find the hole to be a pleasant experience.

No doubt the particular qualities and characteristics of each detention center vary from camp to camp, but you can count on certain similarities. With few exceptions, you will be locked down in your cell all day long, except for one hour of exercise in a cage roughly the size of your cell, and you will be allowed out for a shower at least every other day. Other than those occasions, your only contact with other humans will be confined to monosyllabic communications with the guards who supervise your movements, and occasional exchanges with the orderlies who bring your food. Usually the hole is a place for solitary confinement, but perhaps you will share a cell with another convict, in which case you will be able to talk with him.

Depending on which camp hole you're in, it's more than likely you won't have any fresh air, and the thermostat that regulates the temperature and air flow in your cell will not be the same ones used in the NASA space programs. You will be hot and cold for inexplicable reasons, and you won't be adequately equipped to make yourself warmer or cooler. In some severe cases, where the transgression is deemed serious, you will be stripped naked, and housed in a cell with no bedding, toilet paper, toothbrush or toothpaste, reading material, or any running water except that in your toilet bowl.

You are supposed to be allowed to use the phone once a week, but whether or not you get to, more often than not, will depend on the disposition of the guards and what they think of you or have been told to think of you. The hole is, in addition to being a holding tank during internal investigations, used as the physical setting for behavior modification and "attitude adjustment." I had the harrowing experience of hearing one guard answer another's question as to what so and so was in the hole for with, "He's here for an attitude adjustment! Haw, haw!" This was clearly guardese for, "We're going to make him so miserable he'll definitely think twice before he pulls that crap again."

Stays in the hole range from one day to forever, depending on the severity of your infraction, the intentions of your jailors, and the attention of your lawyer. If you have pissed off the wrong people, you can count on an experience of indeterminate length, and a wide range of mental (and sometimes physical) abuse. Many of the guards view supervising your time in the hole as a mandate for inflicting additional aggravation in your life, as well as an opportunity to work out any lingering frustrations they can't shed by simply kicking their dogs or abusing their wives and children. Your helplessness seems to bring out the fascist bully in them.

On the other hand, some convicts enjoy the hole, viewing it as a respite from the demands of camp life and the burden of communication with other convicts. To them, the hole is a place they can sleep all day and masturbate in privacy if they so choose, a place where they don't have to make their bed or stand for count — in effect, a mini-vacation.

THE END

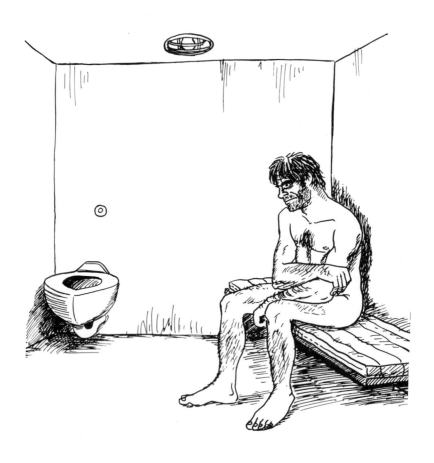

ONE LAST WORD

You will have a lot of time on your hands. Improve yourself. Learn to type. Learn a second language. Learn from the experiences of other convicts. Work out and exercise. And remember... statistics show that just about all of us will be joining you soon, so make plenty of that Inmate Dip.

GLOSSARY

A&O: Admissions and Orientation

BOP: Bureau of Prisons

Camp Wannabe: Name given to prison camps because the inmates make up stories about their backgrounds

Cop-Out Sheet: Official Name: "Inmate Request To Staff Member"

Diesel Therapy: Being transported on the Silver Bullet

Down: In prison

FPC: Federal Prison Camp

Gig: A minor "shot." Four gigs equal one shot

Going Down Further: Being shipped to a higher level prison

Hack: Guard. Prison Officer

Hole: Isolation cell for punishment

Home: Your cubicle where you live

Inmate Dip: A treat made by inmates. See page 73

Leg Rider: An inmate who interacts excessively with a staff person and does so in an obviously servile, obsequious manner, hoping to gain some favor.

New Law: Crime committed after October of 1987. 85% of sentence must be served

Old Law: Crime committed before October of 1987. One-third of sentence must be served

PSI: Presentencing Interview

PSR: Presentencing Report

R&D: Receiving and Departing

R&G: Roads and Grounds crews

Re-Enlisting: Being sent back to prison for another term.

Shipped: Sent from prison camp to a prison

Shot: A disciplinary action against you for an infraction of the rules. ("The hack gave me a shot for smuggling amino acids into the camp.")

Short: More than half of your sentence has been served

Short Line: You get to eat before the general population

Silver Bullet: Prison bus

Suicide Squad: In higher-level prisons, inmates who watch the new inmates around the clock so that they don't commit suicide

Supervised Release: Parole for inmates under New Law

Town Meeting: Administration talking to general population all at once

"We Got Them By The Balls Now": Inmate phrase used as a joke

YOU WILL ALSO WANT TO READ:

☐ **40083 YOU ARE GOING TO PRISON**, *by Jim Hogshire.* This is the most accurate no-bullshit guide to prison life we have ever seen. Topics covered include: Custody (cops, jail, bail and more); Prison (weapons, jobs, hustles, drugs and the most detailed information on rape in any prison book); Jailhouse Justice (segregation, grievances, lawsuits, and more); Execution (death row, "death watch," lethal injection, gas chambers, hanging, electrocution, and more.) If you or a loved one is about to be swallowed up by the system, you need this information if you hope to come out whole. *1994, 5½ x 8½, 175 pp, index, soft cover.* **$14.95.**

☐ **76041 THE OUTLAW'S BIBLE**, *by E.X. Boozhie.* The best "jailhouse" law book ever published — for people on the outside who want to stay there. This is a real life civics lesson for citizen lawbreakers: how to dance on the fine line between freedom and incarceration, how to tiptoe the tightrope of due process. Covers detention, interrogation searches and seizures. The only non-violent weapon available for those on the wrong side of the law. *1985, 5½ x 8½, 336 pp, index, soft cover.* **$16.95.**

☐ **40071 THE BIG HOUSE, How American Prisons Work**, *by Tony Lesce.* This book is a thorough examination of how the prisons work: how do you house, feed, and control thousands of violent, angry people. It examines the prison system from all sides: the inmates, the guards, the politicians, the taxpayers. And it takes a gritty look at issues like capital punishment, psychosurgery, riot control and dealing with the sexual needs of prisoners. *1991, 8½ x 11, 184 pp, illustrated, index, soft cover.* **$19.95.**

Loompanics Unlimited
PO Box 1197
Port Townsend, WA 98368

FPC7

Please send me the books I have checked above. I have enclosed $_____ which includes $4.95 for shipping and handling of the first $20.00 ordered. Add an additional $1 shipping for each additional $20 ordered. Washington residents include 7.9% sales tax.

Name _____

Address _____

City/State/Zip _____

VISA and MasterCard accepted. 1-800-380-2230 for credit card orders *only.*
8am to 4pm, PST, Monday through Friday.

YOU WILL ALSO WANT TO READ:

YOU WILL ALSO WANT TO READ: